The Guide to Franchising

Other Titles of Interest

HUSSEY, D.
Introducing Corporate Planning
Corporate Planning: Theory and Practice

EILON, S.
Aspects of Management
Management Control

DONALD, A. G.
Management, Information and Systems

The Guide to Franchising

BY

M. MENDELSOHN
Solicitor

SECOND EDITION

PERGAMON PRESS
OXFORD · NEW YORK · TORONTO

SYDNEY · PARIS · FRANKFURT

U.K.	Pergamon Press Ltd., Headington Hill Hall, Oxford OX3 0BW, England
U.S.A.	Pergamon Press Inc., Maxwell House, Fairview Park, Elmsford, New York 10523, U.S.A.
CANADA	Pergamon of Canada Ltd., 75 The East Mall, Toronto, Ontario, Canada
AUSTRALIA	Pergamon Press (Aust.) Pty. Ltd., 19a Boundary Street, Rushcutters Bay, N.S.W. 2011, Australia
FRANCE	Pergamon Press SARL, 24 rue des Ecoles, 75240 Paris, Cedex 05, France
FEDERAL REPUBLIC OF GERMANY	Pergamon Press GmbH, 6242 Kronberg-Taunus, Pferdstrasse 1, Federal Republic of Germany

First edition 1970

Second edition 1979

British Library Cataloguing in Publication Data
Mendelsohn, Martin
The guide to franchising. – 2nd ed.
1. Franchises (Retail trade) – Great Britain
I. Title
658.8'4   HF5429.6.G7   78-40961

ISBN 0-08-022466-0

Printed in Great Britain by William Clowes & Sons Ltd Beccles

TO PHYLLIS PAUL AND DAVID

Contents

Contents

Foreword

PERHAPS one of the least understood industries in this country today, and yet one having enormous growth potential and offering tremendous opportunity to the individual, is franchising.

In this book Mr. Mendelsohn has given his readers a very clear understanding of the subject and I am sure that the knowledge that he imparts will assist the development of franchising in the United Kingdom.

The individual who is at the crossroads of life and has to make a decision as to his future direction would do well to read this book and understand the subject of franchising, since franchising offers such a person a golden opportunity to become his or her own master under the protection of a well-established business format, thereby avoiding many of the pitfalls of starting a new business venture on one's own.

Those of us who have many years' experience in this exciting industry have a saying that embraces the concept of franchising. It is: "On your own, but not alone."

I hope you too will obtain from this book the fervent desire to become part of the franchise industry, but if it does no more than give you a better understanding of franchising it will have served its purpose.

KEITH TARRY
Chairman
British Franchise Association

Introduction to the Second Edition

SINCE the first edition of this book was published in 1970 there have been many developments in the field of franchising in the United Kingdom. Indeed, it has become much more prevalent with the major part of the increased growth occurring within the last three to four years. It seems poised at the present time to enter a period of widespread growth.

In the first edition I made a strong plea for the establishment in the U.K. of a trade organisation. This has now occurred and you will find in Appendix A of this edition an extensive explanation of the aims, objectives, and procedures of the British Franchise Association so that its role may be assessed by those who will have contact with it.

I have extensively revised the chapter on "The Meaning of Franchise—Franchising" and included the definition of franchising which has been adopted by the British Franchise Association. I have also enlarged the chapter on "Franchising in Action" so as to embrace a wider field, and each of the eight founder members of the British Franchise Association has been kind enough to participate in this aspect of the book.

I have decided to drop the chapter of the first edition dealing with "Franchising in the U.K.—What Next?" Various other sections of the book have been updated and, where necessary, re-written and expanded.

I am grateful to Dr. John Stanworth of the Polytechnic of Central London who has recently carried out a field study on three of the companies whose franchises I feature in Chapter 11. Dr. Stanworth has prepared and contributed the Appendix, summarising the results of his interviews with the respective franchisees of these companies. The statistics set out in Appendix B are, as far as I am aware, the only reliable statistical figures available concerning franchising in the U.K. and, as will be seen on reading them and the comments I make in Chapter 11, they provide a very interesting insight into attitudes. In the wider sphere, despite the relatively small sample, these figures provide confirmation of many of the theoretical justifications for franchising that have hitherto been expounded.

I should like to express my gratitude to the following individuals and their companies for granting me interviews, where necessary, and for the contributions they have made to this book: John Lawrence of Budget Rent-a-Car; David Taube and John Gooderham of Dyno-Rod; John R. Corson of Holiday Inn; David Acheson of Kentucky Fried Chicken; Edwin Thirwell and John L. Scott of Prontaprint; Brian A. Smith of ServiceMaster; Hugh Arthur of Wimpy; Keith Tarry and Peter J. Dunscombe of Ziebart; The British Franchise Association; Tony Jacobsen; Christine Jacobsen (Secretary of the British Franchise Association).

I am again indebted to my secretary who has coped so well with my handwriting and with the typing of manuscripts. Ann Harris has prepared the revised index and I am grateful to her for her expert help.

Introduction to the First Edition

FRANCHISING is an industry which has achieved a phenomenal growth rate in the U.S.A. and is now beginning to gain ground in the U.K. I feel that it will in due course achieve a rapid growth rate in the U.K. despite the many misgivings that some people have.

These misgivings arise out of a misunderstanding of the basic philosophy underlying this particular method of doing business. Also an element of mystery that seems to be attached to the use of the word "franchise".

This book is an attempt to break down and analyse what franchising amounts to. Its aim is to provide a quick ready reference guide to the basic principles. It must be appreciated that the scope of this book does not permit a study in depth of the various aspects of a franchise transaction. Indeed, many chapters in this book could form the basis of a separate study.

There are many people to whom I am indebted for assistance with the preparation of this book. My Partners, Bruno Marmorstein, Geoffrey Jacobs, and Bob Patten for their help and encouragement; and Bob Rosenberg of Dunkin' Donuts of America for reading my manuscript and for his helpful suggestions. I am very grateful to the following individuals and their companies for granting me interviews and for the contributions they have made to this book: Messrs. Acheson, Sharman & Brooks of Pleasure Foods Ltd.; Mr. David Taube of Dyno-Rod Ltd.; Mr. Noel Evison of Five Minute Car Wash Ltd.; and Mr. Leslie Spears of Budget Rent-a-Car.

I am also indebted to Rogers Sherwood of National Franchise Reports of Chicago, U.S.A., for his immediate agreement to my use of information published by him.

My thanks also to Mrs. Ann Harris for the excellent index which she has prepared.

Lastly, but not least, my thanks to my wife, my secretary, and some of the staff at my office who have assisted with the typing of manuscripts at various stages.

CHAPTER 1

The Meaning of Franchise—Franchising

FRANCHISING as a legal or marketing concept is not new. Nevertheless, it is a topic which has aroused suspicion and hostility which it does not deserve. As in many instances where feelings of suspicion and hostility are to be found, lack of understanding is the cause. There is no reason why franchising should arouse any more antagonistic feelings than any other type of business method.

Franchising has developed out of a number of business transactions, methods, and practices that have been common and popularly known for very many years.

Among the basic features of these business transactions, methods, and practices are to be found the following:

1. The ownership by one person of a name, an idea, a secret process, or a specialised piece of equipment and the goodwill associated with it.
2. The grant of a licence by that person to another permitting the exploitation of such name, idea, process, or equipment and the goodwill associated with it.
3. The inclusion in the licence agreement of regulations relating to the operation of the business in the conduct of which the licensee exploits his rights.
4. The payment by the licensee of a royalty or some other consideration for the rights that are obtained.

These features, as will be seen, among others, are also found in every single franchise transaction.

How then did franchising develop into what it now is? To put franchising into its proper perspective it is helpful to consider the well-known transactions that have been with us for so many years and then to compare franchising with them. It is evident, with the benefit of the hindsight we now possess, that franchising has grown or, one may say, evolved, as a consequence of the natural development of those transactions. If this basic point is mastered at this stage it will considerably assist in an understanding of the meaning of franchising.

One of the most common transactions arises out of the invention of some new machinery. The inventor will wish to ensure that he enjoys the fruits of his invention to the full and will as a first step secure his exclusive rights by obtaining a patent.

He may not have the financial resources or the knowledge to achieve the maximum nationwide or, indeed, worldwide exploitation that his invention merits. He may overcome this problem by entering into agreements with others who do have the financial resources and the business acumen to take the best possible advantage of the invention.

Under the agreements he will grant a licence (or permission) to manufacture, sell or perhaps merely to use the invention in return for a capital sum, a royalty or a capital sum in addition to a royalty. This arrangement makes the maximum use of the inventor's skills and know-how, on the one hand, and the financial resources and other abilities of the licensee, on the other hand.

Another common transaction arises out of the coining of a trade mark in relation to certain goods. The owner of the trade mark, for reasons similar to those which motivate the inventor with his patent, will grant a right to others permitting them to exploit the trade mark. The technical name for the agreement employed in such a case is a "registered user agreement" or, if the trade mark is not registered, a "user" agreement. A trade mark user agreement contains provisions which regulate the conduct of the business to be carried on and the standards to be observed in relation to preparation, presentation, marketing, sale, and the quality of the goods. These provisions are necessary to preserve the standards of quality and the reputation associated with the trade mark. So many of the elements of a franchise transaction are found in such an agreement that, for example, the Wimpy franchise contract is in fact a registered user agreement.

On a slightly different plane are those now very common transactions whereby the use of a famous name in entertainment, sports, or even a cartoon strip character is licensed. In each of these cases, by entering into licence agreements the owners of the names and their licencees are both obtaining benefits that would otherwise not be available to either.

There are other transactions designed to benefit licensor and licensee, which are worthy of mention. The appointment of a dealer by a motor-car manufacturer; the appointment of exclusive sales distributors; the licensing of the use of the name of a large oil company on a garage; as to the latter everyone is familiar with the Shell, Esso, Regent, or Mobil station, but no one would think that all garages bearing an oil company's name are necessarily owned by that company. In many cases the rights granted are now commonly called franchises.

These examples demonstrate that franchising is not new and has been evolving over many years.

What, then, is new? First, there is the wider use of the name "franchising" to describe generically "licence-type" transactions. Secondly, there is the "total business" concept whereby a person develops, as will be seen, a complete method for the setting up and conduct of a business, and licences (or franchises) others to trade utilising the particular method.

Clearly, there are many types of transactions entered into "franchise", each having a different application. The differences will be apparent after the main type of franchise has been defined. To avoid confusion the main type of franchise (i.e. the total business concept) will be referred to as a "business format" franchise, which is the name by which it is commonly known.

The business format franchise involves the exploitation not merely of goods identified by a trade mark or an invention, but the preparation of the "blue print" of a successful way of carrying on a business in all its aspects. The blue print must have been so carefully prepared as to minimise the risks inherent in opening any new business. For example:

criteria will have been established by which the suitability of sites available for the positioning of the business will be judged;

the person buying the business will be trained in the business methods that make that business different from other businesses of its type;

he will also be trained in the methods of marketing and merchandising that exploit the merits of the business to the full and one hopes avoids its pitfalls;

he will acquire the right to use the description by which the business is to be distinguished from other franchises, while at the same time the business is recognisable as a part of the larger organisation that comprises him and his fellow franchises;

all this will be spelled out in the blue print.

The seller of the blue print (the franchisor) will have prepared and smoothed the way for a person, who has probably never owned or operated a business before, to open up a business of his own not only with a predetermined and established format but with the backing of an organisation that would not otherwise be available to him, i.e. the backing of an organisation characteristic of the head office of a large corporation without many of the disadvantages. For the acquisition of the franchise and the continuing services that the franchisee will obtain (see below) there will, of course, be a fee payable.

What we have then are the four basic features mentioned on p. 1, namely:

1. The ownership by the franchisor of a name, an idea, a secret process, or a piece of equipment and the goodwill associated with it.
2. The grant of a licence (franchise) by the franchisor to the franchisee permitting the exploitation of such name, idea, process, or equipment and the goodwill.
3. The inclusion in the licence (franchise) agreement of regulations relating to the operation of the business by which the franchisee exploits his rights.
4. The payment by the franchisee of a royalty or other consideration for the rights that are obtained.

But in addition and fundamentally there will always be a continuing relationship which should provide the franchisee with the full support of a comprehensive range of expert knowledge in the operation of his business in the form of the "head office organisation" of the franchisor.

There have been many attempts at a definition of a franchise in the

U.S.A., the home of modern franchising. Most of them seek to provide a short, snappy phrase that has the effect of omitting much that should be included. It is not the function of this book to seek to establish a concise definition, for with understanding of the subject such a definition becomes unnecessary. However, there is at the end of this chapter a summary of the factors that are essentially a part of every business format franchise.

In seeking to achieve understanding it is of considerable assistance to look at the definitions that have been formulated so far. I propose to analyse two such definitions although many others exist, but this first definition appears in the by-laws of the International Franchise Association (the IFA) which is the trade association of the American franchise industry:

> A franchise operation is a contractual relationship between the franchisor and franchisee in which the franchisor offers or is obligated to maintain a continuing interest in the business of the franchisee in such areas as know-how and training; wherein the franchisee operates under a common trade name, format and or procedure owned or controlled by the franchisor, and in which the franchisee has or will make a substantial capital investment in his business from his own resources.

This definition is concise and quite comprehensive, yet at the same time it poses questions rather than provides answers. The real meaning is hidden in the significant yet apparently innocent phraseology. For example, it refers to the franchisee making an investment in his own business yet nowhere does it say that the franchisee must own his own business. This point which is a fundamental feature of a franchise is implied rather than asserted. As excellent as this definition is, it will be far better understood by those who already have a working knowledge of franchising the type of transaction; it is not for those who seek an underlying understanding.

There are a number of significant phrases in the I.F.A. definition and each will now be examined in turn.

1. *"A franchise operation is a contractual relationship."*

Let us clearly establish at once that a franchise is a contract—just like buying a bar of chocolate is a contract. It is in no way different from any other contract in that the terms upon which the contract is made are expressed in the contract. Perhaps it is just that bit more important that a franchise contract contains each and every term that has been agreed, for it is a contract with which the parties are going to have to live for a very long while. Moreover, it is going to be the provider of bread and butter, and perhaps a little jam, to the franchisee or perhaps the sole provider, so that any material omission may alter the whole course of his life.

2. *"The franchisor offers or is obligated to maintain a continuing interest in the business of the franchisee in such areas as know-how and training."*

One will have to excuse the American "obligated" instead of obliged, but perhaps one should not excuse them for having put the cart before the horse. Of course the franchisor must maintain a continuing interest in the franchisee's business, but first, at least, get the business started. This is the first point that is omitted from the definition.

It is the franchisor's obligation to introduce the franchisee to and initiate him in the business which he will be acquiring.

It is the franchisor's obligation to decide responsibly whether the prospective franchisee is in fact the right sort of person for that particular type of franchise. Nothing could be more disastrous for both parties than to place a square peg in a round hole.

It is the franchisor's responsibility to introduce the franchisee to all relevant areas of know-how for the conduct and operation of the business by pre-opening training.

Know-how as a term is meaningless until one defines what is intended to be included in the expression. It will, of course, differ from case to case. Before the franchisee opens for business this vital part of the blue print which he is being sold must be given to him. Know-how covers suitable business organisation, merchandising as applied to the particular operation, application of the principles of business management appropriate to the nature and type of business, operational methods, introduction to the franchisor's secret and confidential systems, methods, and in some cases formulae. The franchisee must be fully trained in all these aspects before he is let loose in his own business, and when he is he should have any necessary on-the-spot opening help in getting off the ground.

Having reached this stage, the franchisee should have a full grasp of know-how applicable to that particular business; the franchisor should continue to maintain these services coupled with the provision of a trouble shooter to assist his franchisee through his difficulties and promotional assistance to help maximise the beneficial exposure of the operation to the public to the mutual advantage of franchisor and franchisee.

3. *"Wherein the franchisee operates under a common trade name, format and/or procedure owned or controlled by the franchisor."*

This brings us to the crux of the matter. This relates to the central feature around which the blue print is developed. To put this into more practical terms it is helpful to refer to the "Wimpy" franchise. In that case the common trade name is Wimpy, the common format is the identical nature of the business carried on by all the Wimpy franchisees wherever they are. Included in this format are the similar shopfronts, the similar shopfittings and decor, even menus and menu cards. The procedure common to all Wimpys is the preparation of the food and the identical nature of the Wimpy one would buy in any Wimpy store in any part of the country.

This part of the definition refers to those matters which constitute the basic operation and by which the public clearly identifies the individual operation as being part of a larger group of similar operations while, of course, the operation and all its counterparts have the advantage of being run on a day-to-day and involved basis by its owner and not a manager.

The fact that the trade name, format, and the procedure are owned by the franchisor and used by all franchisees in common with each other is what makes an element of control over the franchisees' business essential. Whatever degree of control is exercised by the franchisor over any franchisee should not be looked at by that individual in the light of his reaction to his own involvement. He is too close to the problem. To put it into the correct perspective the only way he can fairly consider the matter is to appreciate that the franchisor and all franchisees are dependent upon each other for their success. A customer lost at one outlet can be a customer lost to all the others also. In effect the franchisor and all the franchisees are presenting a combined operation to the public. As a satisfied customer whose loyalty has been gained by good quality and good service moves about the country he will patronise an operation apparently part of the group that has looked after him well before, rather than a competitor.

4. *"And in which the franchisee has or will have a substantial capital investment in his business from his own resources."*

As mentioned before, the franchisee must own his own business. The franchisee has the right to own the business for which he is paying and he must have the right to sell the equity he has developed in the business.

There may be certain limitations on the exercise of the right to sell; for example, the franchisor may require a right of first refusal or he may require to first vet and train any prospective purchaser to satisfy himself that the purchaser satisfies the basic qualifying standards for a franchise and is not a square peg. It is also possible that the franchisor will have a waiting list of prospective franchisees to whom the business could be offered for sale.

The reference to the capital investment is not superfluous. It is important that a franchisee will make a substantial capital investment from his own resources. This goes a long way in motivating him. A person who has his own money at stake and who can see that he has the opportunity to control the destiny and growth of his asset by his diligent attention to the correct operation of the business will put everything he can into the business and not the half-interest of a manager.

So far there has been no mention of payment. No franchisor is going to give anything away for nothing. If it appears that he is doing so this is something that should be investigated. No one is in business to make gifts of his products or services. The franchisor is no exception to this general rule. Payment is made to the franchisor in any number of ways. He may ask for a franchise fee by name. He may sell a package which has the franchise fee included in the price. He may receive a percentage of the franchisee's takings. Whichever way the fees are to be taken by the franchisor he will be paid both for his initial services and for the continuing service which he provides.

One other factor which must be touched upon at this stage is the problem of territorial rights. This is a subject on which there can be no general rule save that the franchisee must have some guarantees that the area surrounding the site of his operation will not be over-saturated to his detriment. This is a very difficult matter, for some franchised operations will thrive upon a massive saturation of an urban area while others will by their nature require a carefully defined and protected area of operation.

The second definition which is considered relevant is that which has been adopted by the British Franchise Association. The British Franchise Association defines a franchise as:

A contractual licence granted by one person (the franchisor) to another (the franchisee) which:

(a) permits or requires the franchisee to carry on during the period of the franchise a particular business under or using a specified name belonging to or associated with the franchisor; and

(b) entitles the franchisor to exercise continuing control during the period of the franchise over the manner in which the franchisee carries on the business which is the subject of the franchise; and

(c) obliges the franchisor to provide the franchisee with assistance in carrying on the business which is the subject of the franchise (in relation to the organisation of the franchisee's business, the training of staff, merchandising, management or otherwise); and

(d) requires the franchisee periodically during the period of the franchise to pay to the franchisors sums of money in consideration for the franchise or for goods or services provided by the franchisor to the franchisee; and

(e) which is not a transaction between a holding company and its subsidiary (as defined in Section 154 of the Companies Act 1948) or between subsidiaries of the same holding company or between an individual and a company controlled by him.

Apart from the paragraph (e), which clearly has a technical basis, the definition embodies much of the I.F.A. definition which has been analysed above, the following points of comparison will be of interest:

(i) the definition confirms the contractual nature of the relationship;

(ii) it asserts the right or the licence granted to the franchisee to carry on the business, although it does not confirm that the franchisor will be obliged to provide the initial training;

(iii) it deals with the question of control by the franchisor over the manner in which the franchisee carries on the business;

(iv) it confirms the obligation of the franchisor to provide the continuing assistance that is so essential;

(v) it deals with the question of the payment of the franchise fee.

As with all definitions it is one which has been coined for a particular purpose and no doubt it was the intention of the Association to frame its definition on such a basis that membership will be available to companies whose franchise, while not strictly a "business format" franchise, is still a franchise of a more limited nature (see Chapter 4 for a discussion on other types of franchise).

Membership of the Association carries with it responsibilities, and it is clearly in the interests of the Association and of the members of the public that, so long as the business to be conducted is what may be reasonably described as a franchise within the generic sense in which the term is understood in business circles, such a franchisor should have the ability to join the Association. It is significant in fact that the definition omits reference to the initial training in setting up the business, and it is also significant that the definition omits the requirement that the franchisee should have made a substantial capital investment out of his own resources in the business he would operate. The parallels between the two definitions are quite clear, and from these definitions and this discussion emerge the following basic features which must be present in every "business format" franchise:

1. There must be a contract containing all the terms agreed upon.
2. The franchisor must initiate and train the franchisee in all aspects of the business prior to the opening of the business and assist in the opening.
3. After the business is opened the franchisor must maintain a continuing interest in providing the franchisee with support in all aspects of the operation of the business.
4. The franchisee is permitted under the control of the franchisor to operate under a trade name, format and/or procedure, and with the benefit of goodwill owned by the franchisor.
5. The franchisee must make a substantial capital investment from his own resources.
6. The franchisee must own his own business.
7. The franchisee will pay the franchisor for the rights which he acquires in one way or other.
8. The franchisee will be given some territory within which to operate.

Mention has already been made of the fact that there are different types of franchise. This aspect will more appropriately be dealt with in Chapter 4. What one must now consider is how and why franchising works in practice.

CHAPTER 2

How and Why Franchising Works in Practice

ONE fact that is clearly demonstrated in Chapter 1 is that a franchisee opening for business is in a very different position from any other person who does so. The difference arises because of the pre-opening training guidance and preparation for the prospective business and the existence of an organisation to provide the necessary continuing training and guidance while the business is running which the franchisee obtains. This difference and all it involves is one of the two features that lie behind the successful functioning of franchising in practice.

The other feature is the personal involvement of the franchisee as the owner of the business. From the franchisor's point of view it is the difference between dealing with a manager of a branch with all the difficulties of motivation control and responsibility, and dealing with the owner of a business. The motivation and responsibility of the owner of a business should rarely be in issue, particularly if the franchisor's selection methods are good. The problem of control is not eliminated, but the nature of the problem is different.

A person who opens a new business, particularly if he has no previous experience, runs considerable risks. The effect of these risks can best be demonstrated by statistics, but, unfortunately, statistics of the nature required are not available for the U.K. The figures that have hitherto been available for the U.S.A. are not known to be completely reliable.

It certainly appears to be the case in the U.S.A. that the failure rates for franchised businesses are substantially less than the failure rates for non-franchised businesses. This must to some extent account for the remarkable success of franchising in the U.S.A. It is estimated that sales of goods and services through franchised outlets in the U.S.A. in 1978 will amount to a sum in excess of $280 billion and that the number of franchised establishments will be in the region of 468,000 of which more than half are business format franchises.

Even allowing for the differences that exist between the U.S.A. and the U.K., these figures reveal that franchising has achieved great success in the U.S.A. and there is no reason to doubt that proportionately similar success cannot be achieved in the U.K. Furthermore, from inquiries made by the author the overall failure rate experienced by franchisees of reputable U.K. franchise companies is negligible and supports the view that franchising is a markedly safer way for a new business to be launched.

It is reasonable to conclude that reputable franchising does work in practice to a considerable extent in overcoming the risks inherent in any new business venture. There is no real reason to suppose that when accurate statistics do become available in the U.K. they will reveal a substantially different picture from that revealed by the author's inquiries.

When a new business fails or experiences difficulties it can be caused by any number of factors, e.g. lack of adequate working capital, a bad business concept, poor trading position for that type of business, lack of basic essential knowledge, poor controls, failure to recognise the danger signals, and so on. None of the factors within these categories should, of course, apply to a franchised operation. The franchisor's know-how should have ensured that these factors were anticipated and by the provision of his continuing services enabled the problems to be avoided or ensured that they were tackled at the appropriate time.

The other type of factor which involves the suitability or otherwise of an individual for a particular type of business or, indeed, owning any business at all, is one that often will only emerge after business has commenced and the die cast. No matter how careful the franchisor is in his selection of franchisees, in some cases he will not know until this point in time that an individual is inadequate in this respect.

There is a marked contrast between a franchisee and a non-franchisee when the business runs into difficulties.

The franchisee has the franchisor to fall back on: he should be guided by experts and his losses minimised. He should be given the benefit of further training to see whether the problems can be overcome; he should also be given on-the-spot assistance. Lastly, if all else fails the franchisor may buy the business back from him as a going concern or, alternatively, introduce a prospective franchisee from his waiting list who will buy the business at the current market price. It is not suggested that the unsuccessful franchisee will not lose any of his investment at all, but at least steps can and should be taken to assist in mitigating his loss. The author is aware of actual cases where franchisors have helped unsuccessful franchisees to recover their investment which otherwise would have been lost.

How does the non-franchisee stand when he meets his difficulties? Indeed, it is quite likely that without the supporting facilities which the franchisee has available to him he will not even realise for some time that he is trading at a loss. Alas! In many instances too late. Even so, to whom can he turn for advice? His bank manager, his accountant, his solicitor. None of these gentlemen, however skilled, will be able to provide the same guidance as someone who knows his type of business inside out and who can from wide personal experience in that type of business quickly analyse the problem and recommend the appropriate action.

It is suggested that there are three elements present in a franchise transaction that provides the key to the possible success of the franchisor/franchisee relationship.

1. The Preparation of the Franchisee

There are very many men who embark upon a first business venture knowing what they hope to achieve:

> without having had any formal introduction to the basic skills required;
> without any formal training in the management of a business;
> without any experience of the controls that it is essential to introduce to ensure that the business is running on a proper profitable basis, if at all;
> without knowing their way around in their dealings with suppliers and what terms of business to expect;
> without any real idea of what to expect their staff to be capable of achieving; they may not even know what are the proper rates of pay.

There will always be many with whom they will deal who will be only too anxious to part them from their money.

Some of these new businessmen will be successful but very many of them will pay very dearly for the mistakes that they make; their mistakes will be fatal and their business lost before they can apply what they have learned by their experience.

The franchisee, on the other hand, will open for business having been completely and thoroughly trained in all these areas. He will already by his purchase of the blue print have paid for the knowledge and guidance to prepare him so that he will be able to cope with the problems that will arise and hopefully provide the answers.

2. The Continuing Relationship between Franchisor and Franchisee

The franchisee having received all his essential pre-opening training and having been assisted in opening is not then left to himself. He should have the assistance of a trouble shooter from the franchisor's head office behind him. If this head office is functioning correctly it should be giving the franchisee the benefit of the cumulative experience of all his fellow franchisees. This experience would invariably be presented to the franchisee in well-collated training, instruction, and operating manuals. The franchisee is thus learning by the practical experience and innovations of others and also making his own positive contribution to both his own and his fellow franchisee's success.

There are four elements in this relationship. The franchisor provides:

(a) the trouble shooter;
(b) the head office organisation which would not otherwise exist;
(c) manuals recording the training guidance and advice he has given the franchisee;
(d) marketing and promotional advice and innovation.

The franchisor and the franchisee have a mutual interest in the franchisee's success. The franchisee's interest is obvious—it is his own business. The franchisor wants the franchisee to succeed because it will help his own successful growth.

The franchisor's trouble shooter should contact the franchisee even if not asked to call. He will be concerned not only with any problems which the franchisee has but with ensuring that the franchisee maintains the necessary standards. He may be able to spot a problem before it has developed to the point of causing trouble or before the franchisee has noticed it.

The trouble shooter should be backed by a head office organisation with specialists in the various fields in which the operation is involved. Examples of the fields which the experts might cover are:

> advertising and merchandising;
> product innovation and quality control;
> business methods and equipment.

These experts can be called in to assist, and it may be that in obtaining the solution of the problems met by one franchisee the same problem can be avoided or mitigated for all other franchisees.

It is said that necessity is the mother of invention; a franchisor under the pressure of having to help an ailing franchisee succeed may have to experiment and thus develop his blue print still further and introduce improvements and refinements much more rapidly than would otherwise be the case.

The manuals with which the franchisee would be provided should contain a record of the initial training received. They would also contain advice on how to deal with situations that arise in practice, e.g. what to do if equipment breaks down and whom to contact. Supplements should be produced from time to time to keep all information up to date as equipment and methods are changed or improved upon.

3. The Franchisee Owns the Business

This is what makes the franchisee work harder and better than a manager; he will receive the benefit of the increase in the value of the equity in the business. Indeed, there are many instances where franchisees have opened and developed a franchised business and sold it. The profits made in effecting such a sale have been quite remarkable and in some cases quite substantial. There will always be a ready market for the ethical and well-run franchised business, not only through its franchisors but also on the open market where the attractions of buying in to a demonstrably successful business under a nationally known brand name are obvious.

Thus a considerable incentive exists for the franchisee, for he knows that the greater the success of his business operation the more money he will put in his own pocket.

For the franchisor, although he will probably earn less from a franchised outlet than from a managed branch, he has far fewer problems. It is not his worry if staff fail to turn up, he does not have to employ them or control them; he does not need vast capital sums to finance the growth or development of his outlets, and he is not critically involved in the day-to-day management problems.

These factors combine to provide a support organisation for the franchisee to ease him through the problems of opening and running his business. If the incentive and application of the franchisee is added it is seen that a very powerful partnership has been created to ensure so far as is humanly possible that the operation will work to the maximum advantage of franchisor and franchisee.

Franchising is not the answer for everyone; it has its advantages and disadvantages. These are considered in the next chapter and will assist in the formation of a balanced view of the overall picture.

CHAPTER 3

The Advantages and Disadvantages of Franchising

A PROSPECTIVE franchisee is going to become a businessman capable of making decisions, and before embarking upon his venture he has to make two vital decisions. The first of these decisions is whether or not to embark upon a franchised business. The second is what particular business to select.

In making a decision about the former, an assessment has to be made of the advantages and disadvantages of franchising from the franchisee's point of view compared with a non-franchised business.

Many of the advantages have been touched upon in the previous two chapters, but it will be useful to summarise them again.

Advantages to the Franchisee

1. The franchisee's lack of basic or specialised knowledge is overcome by the training programme of the franchisor.

2. The franchisee has the incentive of owning his own business despite the background of assistance from the franchisor. He is an independent businessman within the framework of the franchise agreement and can by his own hard work and effort maximise the value of his investment.

3. The franchisee's business opens with the benefit of a name and reputation (a brand image) and goodwill which is already well established in the mind and eyes of the public.

4. The franchisee invariably requires less capital than is required in setting up independently by reason of the assistance given by the franchisor. However, many franchised businesses are organised in a highly sophisticated way, and a franchisee may well have a larger investment to make than he would if he were to open for business without

the franchise umbrella. On the other hand, a more modest investment may jeopardise the success of the business.

5. The franchisee should (where appropriate) receive assistance in:

(a) site selection;
(b) preparation of plans for remodelling the premises, including the obtaining of any necessary town planning or by-law consents;
(c) obtaining finance for the acquisition of the franchised business;
(d) the training of his staff;
(e) purchase of equipment;
(f) selection and purchase of stock;
(g) getting the business open and running smoothly.

6. The franchisee receives the benefit on a national scale (if appropriate) of the franchisor's advertising and promotional activities.

7. The franchisee receives the benefit of the bulk purchasing and negotiating capacity of the franchisor on behalf of all the franchisees.

8. The franchisee has at his fingertips the specialised and highly skilled knowledge and experience of the franchisor's head office organisation in all aspects of his business while continuing in a self-employed capacity.

9. The franchisee's business risk is reduced. However, no franchisee should consider that because he is coming under the umbrella of the franchisor that he is not going to be exposed to any risk at all. Any business undertaking involves risk, and a franchised business is no exception. To be successful, the franchisee will have to work hard, harder than ever before perhaps. The franchisor will never be able to promise great rewards for little effort. The blue print of a way in which to carry on business successfully and profitably can rarely be the blue print to a way of carrying on business successfully without working.

10. The franchisee has the services of trouble shooters provided by the franchisor to assist him with the many problems that may arise from time to time in the course of business.

11. The franchisee has the benefit of the use of the franchisor's patents, trade marks, trade secrets, and any secret process or formulae.

12. The franchisee has the benefit of the franchisor's continuous research and development programmes designed to improve the business and keep it up to date.

13. The franchisor obtains the maximum amount of market infor-

mation and experience which is circularised for the benefit of all the franchisees. This should give him access to information which would not otherwise be available to him.

14. There are also usually some territorial guarantees to ensure that no competitive franchisee is set-up in a competing business within a defined area around the franchisee's business address.

Disadvantages to the Franchisee

1. Inevitably the relationship between the franchisor and franchisee will involve the imposition of controls. These controls will regulate the quality of the service or goods to be provided or sold by the franchisee. It has been mentioned previously that the franchisee will own his own business. He will; but he must accept that for the advantages enjoyed by him, by virtue of his association with the franchisor and all the other franchisees, control of quality and standards is essential. Each bad franchisee has an adverse effect not only on his own business, but indirectly on the whole franchised chain of businesses and all other franchisees. The franchisor will therefore demand that standards are maintained so that the maximum benefit is derived by the franchisee and indirectly by the whole franchised chain from the operation of the franchisee's business. This is not to say that the franchisee will not be able to make any contribution or to impose his own personality in his business. Most franchisors do encourage their franchisees to make their contribution to the development of the business of the franchise chain and hold seminars and get togethers to assist in the process.

2. The franchisee will have to pay the franchisor for the services provided and for the use of the blue print, i.e. franchise fees.

3. The difficulty of assessing the quality of the franchisor. This factor must be weighed very carefully by the franchisee, for it can affect the franchisee in two ways. Firstly, the franchisor's offer of a package may well not amount to what it appears to be on the surface. Secondly, the franchisor may be unable to maintain the continuing services which the franchisee may need in order to sustain his efforts.

4. The franchise contract will contain some restrictions against the assignment of the franchised business. This is a clear inhibition on the franchisee's ability to deal with his own business but, as with most of the

restrictions, there is a reason for it. The reason is that the franchisor will have already been most meticulous in his choice of the franchisee as his original franchisee for the particular outlet. Why then should he be any less meticulous in his approval of a replacement? Naturally he will wish to be satisfied that any successor of the franchisee is equally suitable for that purpose. In practice there is normally very little difficulty in the achievement of successful assignments of franchised businesses.

5. The franchisee may find himself becoming too dependent upon the franchisor. This can affect him in a number of ways; for example, he may not achieve the motivation that is necessary for him to work and build his business to take full advantage of the foundations that the blue print provides.

6. The franchisor's policies may affect the franchisee's profitability.

7. The franchisor may make mistakes of policy; he may make decisions relating to innovations in the business which are unsuccessful and operate to the detriment of the franchisee.

8. The good name of the franchised business or its brand image may become less reputable for reasons beyond the franchisee's control.

These, then, are the advantages and disadvantages which every franchisee must weigh up and consider before making the decision on whether or not he wishes to enter into a franchised business.

He must decide whether the advantages, with the training and support that they provide, are worth having in return for the surrender of independence to the degree of outside control which a franchise transaction entails. He must decide whether his franchisor is the right person with whom to do business; he must decide whether he is personally and temperamentally suitable for the type of relationship that a franchise involves.

Having weighed up all the factors and taken proper professional advice so that he may be sure that each factor has been properly investigated, the final decision rests with the franchisee. If he is not able to take this decision with confidence and by himself after having heard all that his advisors have to say, it may well be that he should consider whether he is the sort of person who is capable of running his own business.

From what point of view, then, should a prospective franchisor approach the position? What are the advantages to him of franchising as opposed to building, developing, and operating his own chain?

Advantages to the Franchisor

1. A small, central organisation which consists of a few highly skilled experts in the various aspects of the business with which the organisation is concerned can earn a reasonable profit without becoming involved in high capital risk in the day-to-day detail and problems that arise in the management of small retail outlets.

2. There is not the need for injections of vast amounts of capital to achieve a rapid growth rate. Each outlet that is opened utilises the financial resources of the individual franchisee.

3. It follows quite logically, therefore, that such an organisation has an ability to expand more rapidly on a national or, indeed, international basis using a minimum of risk capital.

4. It will also be easier to exploit areas, which are not already within the scope of the organisation, as franchisees with local interests and knowledge can be obtained.

5. A franchisor has less staff problems with which to cope as he is not involved in the staff problems of each individual outlet.

6. The local management of each franchised outlet will be keen, well motivated, and extremely alert to minimise costs and to maximise sales: much more so than would be the case with a manager.

7. A franchisor can achieve wider distribution and ensure that he has "tied" outlets for his services and products. This is particularly the case in a franchise organised in the way, for example, that the Wimpy franchise is. Each Wimpy franchisee has to buy his Wimpy and certain other items from his franchisor. No other product that he can obtain anywhere on the market can be described as a Wimpy. Any attempt to do so would be an infringement of the franchisor's trade mark and a breach of the franchise agreement.

8. Certain types of franchise schemes such as the Dyno-Rod drain-cleaning franchise are able to more easily handle accounts on a national basis. There are many organisations which require the services offered by Dyno-Rod who are able to negotiate with large industrial concerns having a number of factories and premises throughout the country arranging for each local franchisee to handle the work that arises on the premises of that company within his franchised area. None of the franchisees would have the ability or the capacity to negotiate or service

arrangements of this nature on his own, yet the group as a whole has the capacity to do it, and each franchisee by the service that he provides to the franchisor's customer ensures that the group as a whole retains the business of the large national company.

Disadvantages to the Franchisor

1. The franchisee very often and very quickly develops a feeling of independence; he is being successful; his business is running well and he is earning what he was told he could expect to earn or perhaps even more. He tends to wonder why he needs the franchisor at all. He becomes convinced that the reason for his success is that he is running his business well on his own initiative. This is a big problem for the franchisor. After all he may be doing his job well and helping his franchisee achieve success only to find that the franchisee now thinks that he is the person who was responsible for his success and that the franchisor is superfluous to his requirements. This is a matter that requires careful handling and skilled supervision.

2. A franchisor has to be on his toes to ensure that standards of quality, services, and goods are maintained throughout the franchised chain. His trouble shooters will act as supervisors of these standards as well as doing their trouble shooting.

3. There is the franchisee who is not alive to the opportunity with which his business presents him. This again is a matter for careful handling by the franchisor, for the franchisor must never forget that the franchisee does own his business. The franchisee has to be educated and coaxed into accepting that the franchisor's suggestions on which action is needed do amount to sound advice. It is not the same thing as saying to the manager of a business "it is now company policy that so and so should be done and therefore you must do it". The franchisee can never be treated in this way. If the franchisor's reasoning and explanations are good it should be possible for him to make the franchisee see how much more sensible he would be to do what he is advised by the franchisor to do.

4. There may arise a lack of trust between the franchisor and franchisee arising out of the incompatability between the franchisee and the individuals within the franchisor's organisations with whom the franchisee has to deal.

5. The franchisor may feel that by all the work and effort he is putting in to training the franchisee, he is in fact preparing a possible future competitor.

6. The franchisor must be sure that the person selected for the franchise is suitable for the particular type of franchise or, indeed, has the capacity to accept the responsibility of owning his own business. The franchisor owes a great deal to prospective franchisees and to the growth of his own business to ensure that no one who is unsuitable is allowed to take a franchise.

7. There is often difficulty in obtaining the co-operation of the franchisee in decorating and renovating his premises or in enforcing other standards so that the public is always given service in the manner stipulated in the franchise agreement and in a manner consistent with the brand image of the franchisor.

8. Problems can also arise where the franchised business forms part of a larger business which is carried on by the franchisee. The franchisee can find certain interaction and conflicts between the staff of the two types of business which may operate to the detriment of either or both.

9. There is the problem of communication between the franchisor and franchisee. It is vital that each should appreciate the importance of communication. The franchisee should appreciate that the franchisor cannot read his mind; he cannot know what is troubling the franchisee unless the franchisee tells him. Likewise the franchisor should not assume that the franchisee has kept himself up to date. It is for the franchisor to ensure that he has communicated his information to the franchisee.

10. While the headaches are greater, a company-owned unit will be more profitable than a franchised unit.

11. If the franchisee is paying his fees on a royalty basis he may not be fully disclosing his gross income.

12. There may be difficulties in recruitment of persons who are suitable for the particular business.

In summing up the disadvantages with which a franchisor is faced one might say that most of the franchisor's problems of a disadvantageous nature arise from his dealings with the franchisee as an individual and the personalities that are involved. This is a problem with which the franchisor would be faced in running his own business. However, there is a vital and subtle distinction between running his own business and running a franchise business in that the franchisee is running his own business and he will resent having the franchisor trying to run his business for him as if it were merely a branch of the franchisor's company. Each party must appreciate how essential are co-operation and mutual dependence and a tolerance and understanding of the way in which the other thinks.

CHAPTER 4

What Can be Franchised?

AS WILL be appreciated, this work is concerned to a large extent with the business format franchise which is described and analysed in Chapter 1. It has already been explained that there are other types of franchise. Franchise arrangements in the widest use of the word are those transactions in which one person grants rights to another to exploit an intellectual property right involving, perhaps, trade names, products, trade marks, equipment distribution, but not amounting to the entire package that is the essential feature of the business format franchise.

These transactions have involved all levels in the manufacture and distribution of goods or products. Thus we see involved in these wider franchises, manufacturers, wholesalers, and retailers, and a complete interchange between all three levels.

There are thus franchises involving transactions between:

    (a)   manufacturers and wholesalers;
    (b)   manufacturers and retailers;
    (c)   wholesalers and retailers.

There is also a fourth category namely that between retailers and retailers: this category is the one which has possibly contributed more than any other to the explosive development of the business format franchise. This would be in the case where a retail business has been a marked success and the proprietor makes the conscious decision to expand his chain by the franchise route.

In order to illustrate the three categories of transaction there follow examples of the types of arrangement involved in each case.

(a) Manufacturers and Wholesalers

The best-known franchise of this type are, perhaps, the soft-drink bottling arrangements entered into by, for example, Coca Cola and Pepsi Cola.

(b) Manufacturers and Retailers

This category includes some of the oldest of this type of franchise arrangement and is effectively limited to the motor-car industry. Thus we find the arrangements made by the motor-vehicle manufacturers with their network of dealers. We also find the arrangements made between the petrol companies and their filling station proprietors. So many of the elements of the business format franchise are present in these arrangements that they may appear to be quite close to achieving that status. There are within the scope of the petrol companies' arrangements with filling station proprietors, different types of transaction ranging from a licensee or tenant of premises owned by the petrol company to a sales agreement with the owner of the filling station which may or may not be exclusive.

(c) Wholesalers and Retailers

This category is not so clearly capable of identification as being distinctly different from the manufacturers and retailers category. There can really be no reason to differentiate between them except that the franchisor is a wholesaler rather than a manufacturer. These franchises are also not so easy to identify with any we have in the U.K., but they include a hardware store or chemist's shop or perhaps a supermarket. In the U.S.A. the motor-vehicle accessory or spares store is clearly identified within this category.

It will be appreciated that the above categories do include some of the traditional methods and practices described in Chapter 1 as being the ideas from which the business format franchise evolved, namely agencies, distributorships, licensing, and know-how agreements. We shall therefore briefly examine the nature of these arrangements and compare them with franchising.

In the first place there are agencies. What is an agent? An agent is, in fact, a person with either an expressly given authority to act on behalf of another person or one who, by the nature of his relationship with that other person is impliedly authorised to act on his behalf. The authority given may be a special authority which is limited to doing one or two specific acts or it may be a general authority giving the agent unrestricted power to act. Fundamentally, an agent throughout does not act on his own behalf. He acts on behalf of and in the name of his principal. There is no separation of principal from agent in the eyes of third parties dealing with them. Whatever the agent says or does is completely and effectively binding upon his principal. As between the agent and the principal, of course, there are duties that each owes the other, but the third party is not usually concerned with whatever these private arrangements may be.

In all franchise arrangements the parties usually go to great lengths to ensure that no agency relationship arises. Indeed, invariably in franchise agreements there is specifically a provision that the franchisee is not the franchisor's agent or partner and has no power to represent himself as the franchisor's agent or as being empowered to bind the franchisor. Some agreements even require the franchisee to state prominently that he is a franchisee or licensee of the franchisor so that the consumer is in no doubt as to the position.

The expression agency, like the expression franchise, is used quite often in the wrong context. It is, in fact, often used in the context of distribution arrangements. A distributor is, in essence, usually a wholly independently owned and financed wholesale operation which is granted certain distribution rights in relation to a product.

The real relationship between the parties is that of vendor and purchaser. The distributor is a completely independent businessman. Unlike the agent in his dealings he does not bind the person by whom he has been granted the distribution rights. He may carry a range of products in respect of which he has a distribution agreement and he may have competing or conflicting lines. The business he conducts is his own business, and he is no doubt motivated purely by commercial considerations deciding whether or not to accept any restrictions that may be imposed upon him in a distribution agreement. The vendor and purchaser relationship may also be present in a franchise agreement, but in most cases it should only be a feature and not the whole substance of the arrangement.

Licensing and know-how agreements are, invariably, the same thing. A licence is descriptive of the nature of a transaction by which one party authorises another to carry out or perform certain functions. A know-how agreement is a particular type of licence agreement and is most widely to be found in relation to technology transfer. These types of arrangement largely arise out of patent or trade-mark exploitation and will usually authorise the manufacture of a product or a piece of equipment. It is not necessarily the only business carried on by the licensee. He may well be combining his activities under the licence or know-how agreement with many other activities. It may be that the product which is being manufactured under licence is complementary to or an accessory of something else that he does or makes. Alternatively, it may just make a useful addition to his existing range. Again, unlike the agent but like the distributor, he is an independent businessman. He runs his own business; he does not act by or on behalf of the person who granted him the rights. This type of transaction is the closest there is to a business format type of franchise.

How does franchising differ?

Let us take a simple example. Take a company which manufactures meat products which introduces as one of its new lines—a hamburger. Experience shows that the hamburgers sell well and are very popular. Some bright young man in the marketing division says "Why don't we open up our own restaurant to sell our hamburgers?"—so they do.

They could, at that point in time, have decided to get a wider distribution for their product by entering into a licensing agreement with other meat manufacturers for the same hamburger to be manufactured according to the same recipe in various parts of the country or territory with which we are concerned. They may do this in any event. They may have a distribution network of their own or they may distribute through meat wholesalers under distribution agreements.

In this case, however, they have decided in addition to those traditional methods to open up a retail outlet, and they develop a limited menu fast-food operation built around their hamburger. They have provided an additional method of exploitation of their product. They have gone direct into the retail market but the; do not have sufficient or do not wish to commit a large amount of capital to open rapidly a chain of what could prove to be very successful hamburger bars.

So what do they do? They decide to exploit the distribution of the product at retail level by granting franchises or licences to others who will run identical hamburger bars modelled on exactly the same basis as the pilot operation that the manufacturer had set up. The franchisees would trade under the same name which has become established, the same format, the same procedures. They will sell the same product. A consumer should feel on entering each store that it is part of the same organisation and that the service and product is identical in each store. In other words they establish a business format franchise.

The manufacturer has expanded its distribution network; at the same time it is utilising the staff and facilities of its head office by providing a back-up to the franchisees in various stores. It is therefore making a far more economic use of the amount of expertise available in its organisation. A very rapid growth of the retail outlets can be achieved without the franchisor having to make available vast amounts of capital resources which it can ill afford or which it is reluctant to do.

So far as the franchisee is concerned, what is his position? He is certainly not an agent. He is not acting on behalf of the franchisor and he is not binding or committing the franchisor. He is his own man. He owns his business, he is an independent businessman, he puts the necessary capital into the business and he runs it and manages it. He is not a distributor in the ordinary sense, although he is part of the franchise distribution network. His position is not incompatible with a distributorship for he is certainly buying a product and selling it, but he is applying a process to the product before resale. He performs his activities as a principal. He does not have other lines; he is not running any other business independent of this arrangement. What he has got is a complete business concept which is, in effect, being sold to him as a package. So there is a contrast with a distributorship, although there is clearly a common pedigree.

How does this franchise compare with licensing and know-how agreements? In fact the same sort of contrast can be found as exists with the distributorship, although licensing and know-how agreements are even closer relations of franchise transactions than a distributorship. One is inclined to the view that the business format type franchise is directly analogous to the know-how and licensing arrangement. Let us therefore take another look at the franchise arrangement that has been described.

Certainly, there is a licence granted permitting the franchisee to trade under the trade name and in the particular format. There is certainly a know-how agreement. Know-how is imparted in all aspects of the franchised business. Before he is established in business the franchisee will require to be trained in the basic business skills relevant and limited to this particular type of business and in the operational requirements. He will also expect assistance in site selection, design and remodelling of the store, equipment, marketing, and promotion. The franchisee will also expect a continuing interest to be taken in him by the franchisor providing guidance when needed, promotional activities, innovation, and so on. These are the areas in which franchising is providing so much more than the traditional arrangement and which demonstrate the extent of the evolutionary process.

With traditional arrangements the agent, the distributor, or the licensee has his skills and experience which he is making available within the framework of the agency distributorship or know-how agreement. In the franchise arrangement the other party (i.e. the franchisee) does not have the skills, or experience, so he is to be given them and then sustained to the extent that he needs it.

There is also the distribution element in that the franchised retail outlet is part of the franchisor's distribution network but as a retail rather than a wholesale level, which is normally the case with a distributorship.

One element that is missing from the equation is the agency element, and agency is used in the strict sense. In the loose sense in which it is applied to distributorships, it could be said that the franchisee has an agency as well. But certainly no franchisor would want to enter into a franchise arrangement in which the formal relationship between him and the franchisee was that of principal and agent. If that were the case, with all the inherent risks, he might just as well operate his own branch and employ a manager.

Franchising, therefore, is not merely an alternative, it is in reality another weapon in the armoury of the manufacturer, wholesaler, or retailer, which can be utilised to expand his business in addition to the other methods available to him.

It will therefore be appreciated that there is very little that cannot be franchised. Any business that is capable of being run under management is capable of being franchised. This does not mean that any such business will franchise successfully. The successful franchises are usually built round novel concepts, patented equipment, and trade-mark associations. They are invariably novel approaches to an existing concept and, indeed, the food industry demonstrates this factor more readily than most.

A restaurant or a cafe is a class of business that has existed for many years yet, when Wimpy emerged on the market in the U.K. in the 1950s the new type of approach—the limited menu concentrating on doing a little but well—brought immediate success. A further illustration of this point is that in the U.S.A. there are at least nineteen different types of food operation under franchise.

The franchise scheme should aim to fill a gap in the market by providing a service or product that is not readily or at all available. Its introduction should also be timed correctly, for there is no point in introducing a franchised scheme for a service or product which the public have outgrown and do not want or which is on the wane.

The clearest idea that can be obtained of what can be franchised is to examine the experience in practice of others. There have over the years been published many lists and classifications of businesses under franchise in the U.S.A. The following list was published in the first edition of this work and remains valid.

1. Accounting/Tax Services. This embraces tax preparation, computerised accounting systems for specialised professions, small business, and traders.
2. Agribusiness.
3. Art Galleries.
4. Auto Diagnostic Centres.
5. Auto Rentals/Leasing.
6. Auto Supply Stores.
7. Auto Transmission Repair Centres.
8. Auto Washes/Products/Equipment.
9. Automotive Products/Services.
10. Beauty and Slenderising Salons.
11. Building and Construction.
12. Business Aids/Services.
13. Campgrounds.
14. Catalogue Sales.
15. Chemical Maintenance Products.
16. Children's Products/Services.
17. Cleaning/Maintenance/Sanitation Services.

18. Cosmetics.
19. Credit/Collection Services.
20. Dance Studios.
21. Dispensing Equipment (Food and Beverages).
22. Domestic Services.
23. Employment and Temporary Help Services.
24. Entertainment.
25. Food Operations. This category is broken down into nineteen types of operation:
    Barbecue.
    Cantonese.
    Chicken.
    Donuts.
    Fast-Foods.
    Full Menu.
    Hamburgers/Frankfurters.
    Italian.
    Mexican.
    Mobile Units.
    Pancakes/Waffles.
    Pizza.
    Roast Beef.
    Sandwiches.
    Seafood.
    Smorgasbord.
    Speciality.
    Steaks.
    Miscellaneous Food Operations (e.g. Bakery routes).
26. Fund Raising.
27. Glass Tinting.
28. Health Aids/Services.
29. Health Clubs.
30. Hearing Aids.
31. Home Improvement.
32. Industrial Supplies/Services.
33. Lawn and Garden Care.
34. Marketing/Sales Promotion.

35. Motels.
36. Nursing Homes.
37. Office Machines/Systems.
38. Paint/Chemical Coatings.
39. Paint Stripping.
40. Pest Control
41. Pet Shops and Services.
42. Physical Conditioning Equipment.
43. Printing/Duplicating Services.
44. Publishing.
45. Rack Merchandising.
46. Rentals and Leasing (General Equipment).
47. Safety Systems.
48. Sales Training.
49. Schools/Instruction.
50. Scientific Social Introductions.
51. Sewer Cleaning.
52. Signs.
53. Sport/Recreation.
54. Stores (Retail). These include such stores as: dry cleaners; shoe and heel bars; ice cream; bridal salons; jewellers; gift shops; and coin-op laundries.
55. Swimming Pools.
56. Telecopy Systems.
57. Television Systems.
58. Travel Agencies.
59. Tree Services.
60. Vending Operations.
61. Vinyl/Plastic Repair.
62. Water Conditioning Systems.
63. Weight Control.
64. Wigs/Hairpieces.
65. Miscellaneous Products and Services.

Although in its early stages of development with, at the time of writing, twenty-three members, the British Franchise Association's membership already covers the following business classifications.

1. Motor Vehicle Service.
   (a) Rustproofing.
   (b) Car-tuning Service.
   (c) Motor Accessories; Cycles; Cycle Accessories; Camping; Caravaning, and Leisure Goods.
2. Car Hire.
3. Drain and Pipe Cleaning.
4. Printing Shops.
5. Fast Food.
   (a) Fried Chicken.
   (b) Hamburgers.
   (c) Ice Cream Parlours.
   (d) Restaurant/Snack Bars.
   (e) Pizza.
6. Car Rental.
7. Hotels.
8. Bridal Attire Retail Shops.
9. Central Heating and Air Conditioning.
10. Repairing and Recolouring of Vinyl and General Upholstery Service.
11. Soft Drinks.
12. Hairdressers.

A random selection of the franchises listed by the United States Department of Commerce, *Franchise Opportunities Handbook*, results in the following list. The list follows the business type classification in the handbook and comprises some 38 categories compared with the 65 shown on pp.32–34.

Automotive Products/Services

Aamco Automatic Transmissions Inc.	Repair and reconditioning of automatic car transmissions
ABC Mobile Systems	Mobile brake and silencer repairs
Aid Auto Stores Inc.	Retail sales of car parts and accessories

Autocare Corp.	Vehicle repairs, specialising in tuning air conditioning and brake systems
Automation Equipment Inc.	Car-washing equipment
Bou-Faro Co.	Automatic car transmissions repair centres
Cifer Corp.	Distribution of car glass repair products
Collex, Inc.	Accident repair service
Endrust Corp.	Rustproofing
Firestone Tire and Rubber Co.	Tyre sales and service
B. Goodrich Tire Co.	Tyre sales and service
Goodyear Tire and Rubber Co.	Tyre sales and service
Hercules Service Corp.	Rustproofing
Hydro-Sonic Systems Inc.	Mobile truck washes
Insta-Tune Inc.	Car tuning
Kwik Kar Wash	Car-washing service
Maaco Enterprises Inc.	Car spraying
Midas-International Corp.	Exhaust and brake service
Miracle Auto Painting	Car spraying
National Auto Glass Co. Inc.	Car glass installation
Penn Jersey Auto Stores Inc.	Car parts and accessories
Tuff-Kote Dinol Inc.	Rustproofing
Valley Forge Products Co.	Mobile distributors of car parts
Ziebart Rustproofing Co.	Rustproofing

Beauty Salons/Supplies

Edie Adams Cut & Curl	Beauty salons
The Barbers, Hairstyling for Men and Women, Inc.	Men's and women's hairstyling
Hair Replacement Centers	Hair replacement
Magic Mirror Beauty Salons, Inc.	Beauty salon cosmetics

Business Aids/Services

American Dynamics Corp.	Financial advisers

Associated Tax Consultants of America	Computerised income tax returns
Audit Controls Inc.	Collection of overdue accounts
Bartercard International Inc.	Organising the trading of goods and services between businessmen
H & R Block Inc.	Preparation of income tax returns
Business Consultants of America	Business advisory service
Business Data Services Inc.	Financial and management service to business
Business Exchange Inc.	Organising trading of goods between businessmen
Commercial Services Co.	Book-keeping services
Comprehensive Accounting Corp.	Book-keeping services
Computer Capital Corp.	Financial consultants
Computer Servicenters Inc.	Managements services to medical, dental, and veterinary professions
Contacts Influential.	Business directories
Critical Factory Systems Co.	Management consultancy and factoring
Freight Rate Auditors.	Auditing of truck and rail freight bills
Incotax Systems Inc.	Preparation of tax returns
Marcoin Inc.	Business advisory services
Muzak Corp.	Sound systems
National Homeowners Service Association Inc.	Domestic appliance repairs
Nationwide Income Tax Service Co.	Income tax returns for individuals
F & M Enterprises Inc.	Service to introduce newcomers to local businesses and services
Success Motivation Institute Inc.	Management services
Systemedics Inc.	Account management: medical field
Tax Man Inc.	Preparation of income tax returns
Telecheck Services Inc.	Information storage and retrieval

Tele-Valuation Inc.   Auditing systems
T V Facts   Localised television guides
Walkin & Co. Inc.   Accounting, tax, and management
                                   services for companies
Edwin K. Williams & Co.   Advisory and book-keeping services
                                   to small businesses

Camp Sites

Holiday Inn Trav-L-Parks   Camping and service facilities,
                                   accommodation for vehicles
Jellystone Campgrounds Ltd.   Camp sites and motor inns
Kampgrounds of America Inc.   Camping and service facilities,
                                   accommodation for vehicles
United Campgrounds   Overnight camp sites

Car/Caravan/Truck/Rentals

Always Rent a Car System Inc.   Car, caravan, and truck rentals
Ajax Rent A Car Company   Car and truck rentals
Budget Rent A Car Corp.   Rental of new cars
Dollar Rent A Car Systems Inc.   Car and truck rentals, particularly
                                   at airports
Hertz Corp.   Car and truck rentals and vehicle
                                   leasing
National Car Rental System Inc.   Car rental and leasing

Clothing/Shoes

Athletes Foot Marketing Assoc.   Top quality footware and
   Inc.   accessories for athletes
Formal Wear Service   Sale and rental of mens formal clothes
Gingiss International Inc.   Sale and rental of mens formal
                                   clothes
Heel'N Toe Inc.   Women's discount shoe shops

Just Pants	Jeans and accessories shops for teenagers
Knapp Shoe Company	Retail shoe shop selling "Knapp Shoes"
Mode O'Day Company	Ladies clothing shops
Modern Bridal Shoppes Inc.	Retail sales of bridal outfits
Pauline's Sportswear Inc.	Cheap ladies clothing
Sally Wallace Brides Shop Inc.	Retail sale of bridal outfits
Shirt Tales Ltd.	Mens shirts, ties, and accessories
Store Systems Inc.	Retail fashion clothing and sportswear

Construction Services

A-Tech Inc.	Surveying to locate water penetration into buildings
Cluster Shed Inc.	Timber frames for house construction
Eldorado Stone Corp.	Manufacture and sale of "Eldorado Stone" and brick-building products
General Energy Devices Inc.	Distribution of solar heating and cooling equipment
Homewood Industries Inc.	Retailing of system for renovating existing kitchen cabinets
Marble-Flow Industries Inc.	Distribution of simulated marble flooring
Masonry Systems International Inc.	Manufacturing and marketing of masonry panels
New England Log Homes Inc.	Sale of DIY log homes
Peneprime International Inc.	Asphalting of roads and parking areas
Poraflor Inc.	Sale and installation of seamless flooring
Porcelite Enterprises Inc.	Process to repair bathroom suites
Rus-Tique Brick International	Manufacturer of brick

Timberlodge Inc.   Sale of pre-cut redwood homes and
                                         commercial buildings

Cosmetics/Toiletries

Color Me Beautiful Cosmetics   Distributing "Color Me Beautiful"
                                         cosmetics to retail outlets
Syd Simons Cosmetics Inc.   Completely equipped makeup and
                                         skin care studios

Drug Stores

Lag Drug Co.   Co-operative advertising group
Medicine Shoppes International   Retail sale of pharmaceutical
  Inc.   products
Rexall Drug Co.   Retail sale of pharmaceutical
                                         medicinal cosmetic and vitamin
                                         products
Union Prescription Centers Inc.   Retail pharmacies

Education Products/Services

Alphabetland Child Enrichment   Kindergartens
  Centers
Butler Learning Systems   Audio visual training programmes
Dootson Driving Schools   Driving tuition
The Image of Loveliness Inc.   Teaching of improvement course
                                         for women, based on biblical
                                         principles
International Travel Trading   Training prospective travel agents
  Courses Inc.
Leisure Learning Centers Inc.   Educational products
Mary Moppet's Day Care Schools   Day care centre for children
  Inc.
Mind Power Inc.   Speed reading and memory
                                         operation

Nadeau Looms Inc. — Audio visual teaching system for cloth making

Patricia Stevens International Inc. — Educational residential schools

Pre-Schools Inc. — Pre-school nursery education

Teller Training Institutes Inc. — Teaching systems

Employment Services

A–I Personnel Franchise Systems Inc. — Professional, clerical, and technical job placement

Adia Temporary Services Inc. — Temporary white collar and industrial staff placement

Bailey Employment System Inc. — National chain agency for placement of professional and office staff

Business and Professional Consultants Inc. — Placement of professional and office staff

Deck & Decker Personnel Consultants Ltd. — Job placement services

Drake International — Worldwide placement of all staff, permanent and temporary

Dunhill Personnel System — National chain of office and technical staff placement

Fanning Enterprises Inc. — Complete range of personnel placement

Gilbert Lane Personnel Service — Executive and office personnel

Kogen Personnel Inc. — Temporary office and permanent executive and office personnel

Management Search Inc. — Professional and clerical staff

Manpower Inc. — Complete range of temporary staff

National Teacher Placement Bureau Inc. — Placement for teachers out of term time

Norrell Temporary Services Inc. — Temporary office and computer staff

Parker Page Associates Inc. — Specialised executive recruitment

Personnel Pool of America Inc.	Temporary staff
Positions Inc., International	Middle management placement
Republic Personnel Service System	Job placement service
Richard P. Rita Personnel System Inc.	Complete personnel placement service
Sanford Rose Associates Inc.	Job placement service, some specialisation
Snelling & Snelling Inc.	Employment service in white collar and industrial field
Temp Force	Temporary office staff
V.I.P. Personnel Systems Corp.	Permanent executive placement

Equipment/Rentals

Taylor Rental Corp.	Commercial, industrial, and domestic equipment rental
Typing Tigers	Office equipment and furniture rental
United Rent – All Inc.	Domestic appliances and equipment rental

Food – Doughnuts

Country Style Donuts	Coffee and doughnut shops
Dunkin' Donuts of America Inc.	Coffee and doughnut shops
Spudnuts Inc.	Retail doughnut shops

Food – Grocery/Speciality Foods

Baloi's Smokehouses	Retail sale of hickory smoked meats

Barberio Cheese Houses Inc.	Quality and gourmet food shops
The Circle K Corp.	Convenience-type food shops
Cookie Factory of America	Retail sale of biscuits and bakery products
Li'l Shopper Inc.	Grocery shops
Majik Market	Food stores
Mr. Dunderbak Inc.	Delicatessens
Open Pantry Food Marts Inc.	Miniature supermarket
The Southland Corp.	Grocery shops
Swiss Colony Stores Inc.	Delicatessen and European speciality foods
White Hen Pantry Division, Jewel Companies Inc.	Delicatessens and bakeries

Food – Ice Cream/Popcorn/Sweets/Beverages

Baskin-Robbins Inc.	Retail ice cream shops
Carvel Corp.	Retail ice cream shops
Ernie's Wine and Liquor Corp.	Off-licences
Karmelkorn Shoppes Inc.	Popcorn and sweet shops
Main Street Original Ice Cream Parlors Inc.	Old-fashioned ice cream parlour and soda fountains
Mister Softee Inc.	Van sales of ice cream
Swensen's Ice Cream Co.	Retail sale of ice cream from old secret recipe

Foods – Pancake/Waffle

General Franchising Corp.	French restaurants, specialising in crepes
Mary Belle Restaurants	Family style pancake and waffle houses
Perkins Cake and Steak Restaurants	Family style restaurants
Van's Belgian Waffles Inc.	Original Belgian waffles and crepes

Foods – Restaurants/Drive-ins/Take Aways

A & W International Inc.	Drive-in-walk-in restaurants
The All American Burger Inc.	Fast food restaurants
Angelina's Pizza Inc.	Take-away pizza houses
Angelo's Italian Restaurants of Illinois	Italian sit-down and take-away restaurants
Arthur Treacher's Fish and Chips Inc.	Fish and chip shops
Beef-A-Roo Inc.	Fast convenience food restaurants
Big Al's Sandwich Joint Syndicate	"Prohibition-era" style restaurants
Big Daddy's Restaurants	Snack bars
Bonanza International Inc.	"Bonanza sirloin pit" restaurants
Boy Blue Stores Inc.	Yogurt and limited menu stores
Bun 'N' Burger International Inc.	Hamburger take aways
Cape Codder System Inc.	Seafood restaurants
Casey Jones Junction Inc.	"Railway theme" restaurants catering for families with small children
Charlie Chan Fast Foods	Quick service Chinese American foods
Chicken Delight	Sit-down and take-away restaurants
Church's Fried Chicken Inc.	Chicken sit down and take away restaurants
Craig Food Industries	Fast food drive-in service, Mexican
Dairy Cheer Stores	Fast convenience foods and sandwiches
Dairy Sweet Co.	Drive-in and take-away fast food restaurants
Der Wienerschnitzel International Inc.	Fast food, hot dog restaurants
Dino's Inc.	Pizza take-aways
Famous Recipe Fried Chicken Inc.	Chicken take-away and sit down restaurants
Frostop Corp.	"Frostop Root Beers" and limited fast food menus

Golden Chicken Franchises	Fast food chicken, pizza, and seafood take aways
Greiners Submarine Sandwich Stop Inc.	Sandwich bars
Happy Joe's Pizza and Ice Cream Parlours	Pizza and ice cream parlours
The Happy Steak Inc.	Steak houses
Heavenly Fried Chicken Inc.	Chicken restaurants, using company process
Howard Johnson Co.	Full service restaurants
Hush Puppy Enterprises Inc.	Fast food limited menu restaurants
International Blimpie Corp.	Sandwich bars
Italian Fisherman Seafood Restaurant	Steak, seafood, and Italian restaurants
J'S Restaurants International Inc.	Family type restaurants, American and Italian meals
Japanese Steak Houses Inc.	Japanese steak houses
Judy's Foods Inc.	Fast food, Hamburger-type restaurants
KFC Corp.	"Kentucky Fried Chicken" take aways
Lil' Duffer of America Inc.	Fast food drive-in restaurants
Little Caesar Enterprises Inc.	Pizza take aways
London Fish N' Chips Ltd.	Fish and chips sit-down and take-away restaurants
Long John Silver's Inc.	Fast food, wide menu restaurants
Maid Rite Products Inc.	Sandwich bars
McDonald's Corp.	Fast food, Hamburger restaurants
Mister S'getti Restaurant	Spaghetti restaurants
Mom 'N' Pop's Ham House Inc.	Steak houses and family style restaurants
Mr. Pizza Inc.	Pizza restaurants
Mr. Steak Inc.	Steak houses
Nickerson Farms Franchising Co.	Restaurants, gift shops, and petrol station complexes
Noble Roman's Inc.	Pizza restaurants

Orange Julius of America	Fast foods and brand drink "Orange Julius"
Pail-O-Chicken Inc.	Chicken take aways
Pappy's Enterprises Inc.	Fast food family restaurants
Pastrami Dan's Inc.	Self-service sandwich and hot-dog bars
The Peddler Inc.	Steak houses
Pepe's Inc.	"Pepe's Tacos Fast Food Mexican restaurants"
The Pewter Mug	English pubs and restaurants
The Pizza Inn Inc.	Pizza restaurants
Ponderosa System Inc.	Cafeteria-style steak houses
Reaban's Inc.	Limited menu hamburger bars
The Red Barn System	Self-service snack type restaurants
Woodall Enterprises Inc. (Ron's Krispy Fried Chicken)	"Ron's Krispy Fried Chicken" take aways
Shakey's Inc.	Pizza parlours
Sizzler Family Steak Houses	Family steak houses
Stand 'N' Snack of America Inc.	Fast food operation
The Straw Hat Restaurant Corp.	Limited menu family pizza restaurants
Terry's Interstate Inc.	Fast food motorists restaurants
Texas Tom's Inc.	Wide range menu, sit-down, and take-away restaurants
Top Boy Systems Inc.	Self-service drive-ins
The Upper Krust Inc.	Delicatessen style, fast food restaurants
Walt's Roast Beef Inc.	Roast beef sandwich bars
Wendy's Old Fashioned Hamburgers	Hamburger restaurants
Wife Saver	Fast food chicken and seafood restaurants
Winky's Drive-In Restaurants Inc.	Fish and chip shops
Yankee Clipper Inc.	Fish and chip shops

General Merchandising Stores

Ben Franklin Division, City Products Corp.	General merchandise stores
Gamble-Skogmo Inc.	Houseware and car accessory stores
Montgomery Ward	Retail sales from merchandise in "Montgomery Ward" catalogues
United Dollar Stores Inc.	"Bantom Discount Variety" stores

Health Aids/Services

The Diet Workshop	Group weight watching
Fat Fighters Inc.	Weight reduction centres
Medicab International Inc.	Services for the physically disabled
Medipower	Medical aid sales and leasing
Our Weigh Inc.	Group weight watching
Space Age Fitness Centers	Health centres with "Mini Gym Isokinetic exerciser"

Hearing Aids

RCI Inc.	Hearing aids in "Montgomery Ward" retail stores

Home Furnishings

Carpeteria Inc.	Franchising retail carpet outlets
Casro Convertibles	Stores selling studio couches
Chrome Concepts Inc.	Chrome, glass, upholstered furniture, wall decor, and lighting
Crossland Furniture Restoration Studios	Furniture repair services

Decorating Den	Custom-made curtains, carpeting, and wallpaper
Flex-Cote Products Corp.	Re-upholstering
Guarantee Carpet Cleaning and Dye Co.	Carpet and upholstery cleaning
"Jack The Stripper"	Stripping of paint and varnish
Mother Hubbard's Cupboards Inc.	Retailing of kitchen furniture
Siesta Sleep Shop Inc.	Retail sale of bedding
Spring Crest Co.	Retailing of curtains and accessories
Steamatic Inc.	Carpet and upholstery home cleaning service
Vinylife Inc.	Upholstery repairs

Laundries, Dry Cleaning Services

A Cleaner World	Drycleaning and laundry
Best Equipment Co.	Drycleaning and coin-operated laundrettes
Bruck Distributing Co. Inc.	Drycleaning of carpets
Coit Drapery and Carpet Cleaners Inc.	Supply and maintenance of curtains
Comet International Corp.	Quick service laundry and drycleaning
Martinizing	Drycleaning using "Martinizing" process

Lawn and Garden Supplies/Services

Lawn-A-Mat Chemical & Equipment Corp.	Sale of lawn products and maintenance service
Lawn Doctor Incorp.	Lawn-care service
Lawn Medic Inc.	Lawn-care service
Surburban Lawn Services	Garden centre service to the home
Turf-O-Matic Inc.	Lawn-care service

Maintenance/Cleaning/Sanitation Services

ABC Maintenance Development Corp.	Commercial premises maintenance services
Armstrong Building Maintenance Co.	Office and industrial cleaning services
Cleantech Corp.	Carpet and upholstery cleaning
Domesticare Inc.	Complete house cleaning service
Duraclean International	Carpet and upholstery cleaning
General Sewer Service Inc.	Residential and Commercial sewer cleaning
Lien Chemical Co.	Commercial and industrial sanitation service
National Chemicals and Services Inc.	Commercial and industrial lavatory cleaning
National Surface Cleaning Corp.	Equipment to clean exteriors of buildings
Roto-Rooter Corp.	Sewer and drain-cleaning service
Sermac Surface Maintenance Systems	Cleaning and restoration of buildings, internal and external
Sonic Mobile Wash Inc.	Mobile building cleaning service
Sparkle Wash Inc.	National mobile power cleaning for all buildings
Ultrasonic Predictable Maintenance Inc.	Detection of gas, water leaks, and electrical faults
Von Schrader Manufacturing Co.	Cleaning of carpets, furniture, and car interiors

Motels/Hotels

Admiral Benbow Inns Inc.	Motor inns throughout the southeast U.S.A.
American Travel Inns	Motels and motor hotels
Days Inns of America Inc.	Nationwide "budget-luxury" motels and restaurants
Family Inns of America Inc.	Motels
Holiday Inns Inc.	Hotels and restaurants

Ramada Inns Inc.	Hotels and motor hotels
Sheraton Inns Inc.	Hotels
Travelodge International Inc.	Motels

Paint and Decorating Supplies

Davis Paint Co.	Retail paint and wallpaper stores
Mary Carter Industries Inc.	Retail decorating shops

Pet Shops/Guard Dogs

Doctor Pet Centers Inc.	Retail pet shops
Western Metro Guard Dogs Inc.	Sale and rental of guard dogs

Printing

Big Red Q Quickprint Centers	Instant printing and copying services
Creative Copy Cats Inc.	"Copy Cat" instant print centres
Insty-Prints Inc.	Instant litho printing centres
Kopy Kat Inc.	All-equipment package for instant print services
Kwik-Kopy Corp.	Equipment package for printing services
Postal Instant Press	While-you-wait printing operation
Quik Print Inc.	Quick copying of letterheads, envelopes, price lists, etc.

Property

Action Brokers Corp.	Estate agents
Bethom Corp.	Estate agents
Century 21 Real Estate Corp.	Estate agencies for established proven agents

Gold Key Brokers Inc.	Residential and commercial property sales and financial advice
International Real Estate Network	Estate agents
Real Estate One Licensing Co.	Network of estate agents
Realty 1 Inc.	National licensed estate agents
Realty World Corp.	Full service network for estate agents and brokers

Recreation/Entertainment/Travel Services/Supplies

American Safari Corp.	Specialist caravan rentals
Disco Factory	Mobile discotheques
Empress Travel Franchise Corp.	Travel agencies
Fascination Ltd.	Coin operated TV games
Fun Services Inc.	Fun fairs
Go-Kart Track Systems	Go-kart track and concession
Billie Jean King Tennis Centers Inc.	Indoor tennis centres
Miss American Teen-Ager Inc.	Beauty contest promotions
Playboy Clubs International Inc.	"Playboy clubs"
Putt-Putt Golf Courses of America Inc.	Miniature golf courses
Putt-R-Golf Inc.	Miniature golf and baseball batting ranges

Retailing – Not Classified Elsewhere

Bathtique International Ltd.	Speciality shops for cosmetics
Buning The Florist Inc.	Florists
Cloud Nine Gifts and Decorative Accessories	Gift shops
Conroy's Inc.	Florists
Fireplace Shops Inc.	Shops selling fireplaces and accessories and furniture

Flower World of America Inc.	Florists
Golden Dolphin Inc.	"Bath boutique" speciality stores
The Great Frame Up Systems Inc.	D-I-Y picture frames
The Jeweler's Emporium	Wholesale and retail jewellery
Lelly's Drive In Photos Inc.	Photography shops
Little Professor Book Centers Inc.	Book shops and newsagents
Miss Bojangles Inc.	Fashion jewellery
My Workshop Inc.	D-I-Y and custom picture framing
Nelson's Photography Studios	Photographic studios
Open Book Marketing Corp.	Book shops Marketing Corp.
Paperback Booksmith	Book and record stores
Radio Shack	Audio products
The Ringgold Corp.	Retail picture framing and art shops
Speedy Wagon Sale Corp.	Products for handicapped people
Sport Shacks Inc.	Sports shops
Team Central Inc.	Audio and domestic appliance stores
Terra Art	Jewellery, bead, and craft shops
The Tinder Box International Ltd.	Tobacconists and gift shops
Wicks 'N' Sticks Inc.	Candle shops

Security Systems

Crusader Security Corp.	Sale of patented security products
Everguard Fire Alarm Co. Inc.	Fire and burglar alarms
Flashguard Inc.	Burglar/fire alarm systems
The Night Eye Corp.	Sale and installation of burglar and fire alarm systems
Qonaar Security Systems Inc.	Sale and installation of security systems
Rampart Corp.	Sale and installation of security systems
Telcoa	Sale and installation of burglar/fire alarms

Soft Drinks/Bottling

Bubble-Up Co.	"Bubble-Up" concentrate producing a lemon lime drink
Cock 'N Bull Ltd.	Soft drinks manufacture
Dad's Root Beer Co.	"DAD's Root Beer"

Swimming Pools

Blue Dolphin Pools Inc.	Manufacture of swimming pools
Leisure Enterprises Inc.	Sale and construction of "Natures Rock Pool"
Lifetime Pools Inc.	Sale and installation of swimming pools
Sylvan Pools	Servicing, repair, and maintenance of pools

Tools, Hardware

Imperial Hammer Inc.	Sale of industrial hammers, general servicing of industrial plant
Mac Tools Inc.	Tool distributors
Snap-On Tools Corp.	Tools and equipment to garages, by travelling salesmen
Vulcan Tools	Mobile sales of tools

Vending

Ford Gum & Machine Co. Inc.	Chewing gum and sweets from vending machines
S & S Distributors Inc.	Vending machines for "Fruit of the Loom Pantyhose"

Water Conditioning

Chemical Engineering Corp.	Sales, rentals, and servicing of water-conditioning equipment
Culligan International Co.	Water-conditioning equipment for all users
Rainsoft Water Conditioning Co.	Sale and leasing of industrial water treatment equipment
Watercare Corp.	Water-conditioning sales and service
Water Refining Co.	Water-conditioning sales and rental service

Miscellaneous Wholesale and Service Businesses

A & D Custom Products Inc.	Mobile sales of canvas to the boating industry
Advanced Technology Inc.	Metal treatment processes
The Armoloy Co.	Metal coating
The Badgeman Corp.	Production of name badges
Bar-Master Inc.	Manufacture and marketing of drinks dispensers
Consumer Products of America Inc.	Rack merchandising in supermarkets and chemists
Covco	Mobile "factory on wheels" for boat cover repairs or installations
Cusack Electronics Inc.	Manufacture and home sale of television picture tubes
Devone Manufacturing Co. Inc.	Manufacture wholesale and retail of various patented products
Diversified Arts	Part-time distribution of paintings
FDPO (For Divorced People Only) Inc.	Dating clubs
Key Korner Systems Inc.	Locksmiths
Magic Fingers Inc.	Manufacture and sale of "Magic Fingers" relaxation equipment

Nationwide Fastener Systems Inc.	Supply of nuts, bolts, screws, etc., from mobile warehouses
Parking Co. of America	Self-service car parks and garages
Redd Pest Control Co. Inc.	Pest control
Stretch and Sew Inc.	Complete knitting kit and instruction
Tepco Inc.	Air-cleaning equipment
Terminix International Inc.	Pest control
United Air Specialists Inc.	Commercial electronic air cleaners

It will be seen from this random selection how widely franchising has been applied in practice and how limitless the scope appears to be. There has also proved to be room for more than one similar type of business within each classification.

There is a word of caution, however; a prospective franchisee must decide whether he is being offered a franchise at all. A franchise scheme must contain the elements of a franchise as described in the first chapter to qualify as a business format franchise.

A number of business opportunities offered in good faith are often loosely described as "franchise opportunities". Examination of the elements of the transaction by reference to the principles contained in Chapter 1 will assist in reaching a conclusion as to whether or not it is a franchise. The types of business that are likely to be within this category are area distributorships, agencies, and dealerships as described earlier in this chapter. These have certain elements of a franchise, but usually a vital element such as the continuing relationship is almost completely lacking. While these other types of businesses do not amount to a business format franchise they are frequently conceived and developed by the application of the principles upon which such a franchise is based.

New schemes amending and adapting these principles will arise from time to time. This is only natural. It is, however, important that any prospective franchisee should recognise the extent of the services and facilities being offered to him. The fact that a particular business on offer does not amount to a business format franchise does not of itself mean that it is not worthwhile.

The ingenuity of the business man has fully demonstrated the versatility of franchising as a business method.

The ingenuity of the modern business man unfortunately has not been limited to the pursuit of legitimate ethical franchising. Indeed, franchising offers scope for the fraudulent as the transaction involves a continuing relationship. If, therefore, the initial franchise fee is set too high, allegedly to cover some of the continuing services which are never intended to be provided, the scope for fraud is obvious. There developed what has become known as the "pyramid selling" scheme which is also sometimes described as a multi-level marketing scheme.

These schemes involve the sale of distributorships to purchasers who may divide and subdivide them and sell them on to those whom they recruit as sub-distributors. Expansion of these enterprises takes place on the chain-letter principle.

The ostensible object is to build up a sales force which will sell the company's products or services from door to door. In fact, selling the goods or services is difficult; they are usually expensive, and areas are often saturated with other distributors. Selling distributorships is much more lucrative and becomes, effectively, the company's business.

These schemes have been recognised as containing elements which are dishonest and, accordingly, the Fair Trading Act 1973 contains provisions which prohibit pyramid-type schemes. The Act also contains provisions which permit the making of regulations;

(a) to control or prohibit the issue, circulation, or distribution of documents which contain invitations to persons to participate in a scheme; and

(b) prohibiting the promoter of a scheme from performing functions which are vital to the operation of such a scheme, e.g. supplying goods or receiving payment for goods. Regulations have indeed been made under and in accordance with these provisions.

It is important to be able to recognise involvement with a pyramid-type scheme. And obviously before signing any contract or parting with money one should take proper professional advice. But it is a matter for suspicion if one is offered or told that there will be a reward (i.e. payment, supply of cheaper products, or any other disguised benefit) for doing something totally unrelated to the sale of the basic product or service with which the scheme is involved. For example, one may be offered a percentage payment of any sum paid to the promoter of the scheme for recruiting another participant, or for persuading such participant to purchase a higher position in the scheme. Other rewards could include a profit or commission on sales, or the provision of services or training to other participants in the scheme, or a commission on sales effected by other participants in the scheme.

Pyramid-selling schemes have cost, for some unsuspecting people, a great deal of money; there are many legitimate franchises in which to invest without becoming involved in pyramid schemes. No legitimate franchise will do what the pyramid schemes do and that is to promise rich rewards quickly and without hard work. Whatever is being franchised legitimately will offer reasonable prospects of good rewards in return for the hard work and application that is the lot of all successful self-employed businessmen.

CHAPTER 5

Setting up a Franchise

THERE are three basic aspects involved in setting up a franchise which break down as follows:

1. Business concept
2. Pilot operations.
3. Development and marketing of package.

We shall consider each in turn.

1. Business Concept

In order to franchise there must be something worthwhile to franchise. The prospective franchisor will have to start with a business. It may be an existing business or may involve the development of a new business.

If it is an existing business, it may well be that he found it successful but is unable to find the right staff or to raise sufficient capital in order to expand the business as quickly and as successfully as he would wish.

If it is a new business, it may well be that the prospective franchisor has developed the germ of an idea in his mind which he wishes to establish right from the outset with the intention of franchising as soon as he has been able to prove its viability.

Whichever of these courses the prospective franchisor adopts, he will have to satisfy himself that the business concept is one which is suitable and viable as a basis for franchising. This will, of course, depend upon many of the factors which are discussed elsewhere in this work. One thing is certain, if the prospective franchisor is intending to develop an ethical franchise, it must be well tried and tested so that he can demonstrate to the prospective franchisees both the viability of the business and its proven success in varying circumstances. This then brings us on to the second consideration.

2. Pilot Operations

It is essential for the franchisor to set up his own operation, invest his own money in it, and test it thoroughly in practice. It will be necessary and advisable for him to test the operation in a number of different locations so that the widest possible experience into varying conditions can be obtained before a franchise package is finalised.

It is not advisable for a prospective franchisor to set up a business which has no distinctive features. All the successful franchises are to be distinguished from similar business in some way or, to put it in perhaps more down to earth terms, each franchise has its own novel gimmick or element of novelty which distinguishes it from other similar businesses.

The franchisor must experiment with different types of equipment to ensure that the best is utilised and at the most economic price. He must also experiment with the use of staff to ensure staffing levels are properly planned so that the minimum expenditure is incurred on staff. He must also calculate the profitability of the business and where it is appropriate lay down the standards for portion and quality control. He must seek to perfect the product and product range that the business is to market.

While this is going on he will be experimenting with the format, decor, and design of the premises so that the most economic use is made of the space available and the most attractive design is employed.

The prospective franchisor should also by experimentation develop the operational procedures to the point where the maximum benefit is obtained from the most economic use of resources, and at this stage the prospective franchisor should also have an eye to the possible ways in which business procedures can be developed and standardised so that performance of the business can be monitored carefully. While developing this aspect of the business, he should become aware of the areas of weakness that can produce difficulties for the business so that his experience gained in this area can be avoided when the business comes to be franchised.

3. Development and Marketing of Package

The comprehensive preparation of the franchise package will involve the following factors.

It will be necessary for the franchisor to establish the criteria by which sites are to be evaluated for the particular type of franchise which is being marketed. In doing so he will have to take into account a number of factors such as:

(a) the type of street;
(b) the environment;
(c) foot and/or road traffic volumes;
(d) the degree of identification to which the premises are exposed;
(e) land marks and the business that they may generate, e.g. museums, schools, churches, cinemas, and youth clubs;
(f) the growth potential of the area as a developing community;
(g) type of population.

All these factors, of course, may not be relevant for all franchises.

The franchise equipment package has to be compiled. This package will incorporate all the fixtures and fittings which are either essential for the purposes of the franchised business or standardised pieces of equipment which are necessary in order that the corporate format may be presented to the public.

The design and decor of the stores will have to be decided upon and standard layouts prepared. Plans upon v hich applications for planning and by-law consents can be based will have to be made available. These plans will also be utilised for the guidance of the shopfitters.

Operating manuals will have to be prepared giving the franchisee all the information which he will require in connection with the equipment that is being supplied to him, where to get it serviced, whom to contact in the event of any emergency, and any specialised operational information that may be necessary for purposes of the franchisee's business. The manual could be used as an aid in training and as an *aide mémoire* to the franchisee of the items covered in training when he is later in business.

The franchisor will have to decide on the scope of the business and the services that are to be offered to the public, e.g. in a food franchise—the menu; in the retail store—the range of stock.

The franchisor will have to make arrangements with the suppliers of the basic material or goods with which the business will deal for the sale thereof to the franchisee at competitive prices. These arrangements may extend to suppliers of any bags, boxes, and other materials which are utilised at the point of sale.

Arrangements will have to be made with equipment suppliers so that proper supplies are available to meet the franchisee's demand for the equipment and spare parts and that any necessary service facilities are available.

Systems of work will have to be reduced to writing: job descriptions will have to be prepared explaining the scope and all the facets of each employee's activities so as to fit in with the blue print.

Promotional literature including point of sale material will have to be prepared as will any common format literature and notepaper.

The franchisor will have to set up training schedules and training facilities for franchisees where this is appropriate for the particular type of franchise.

The franchisor will have to prepare accounting procedures and business systems which are to be operated by the franchisee in each case. The franchisee will have to be trained in these systems and methods which will operate to fulfil two purposes. Firstly, to ensure that the franchisee has the maximum amount of information available to enable him to see where his operation is going wrong or, if it is going right that it is in fact going right. Secondly, to provide the franchisor with the maximum of information to enable him to keep control of the business in so far as this may be necessary for the purpose of carrying out his trouble-shooting and follow-up service. They will also provide the franchisor with information which he will need to have readily available for the purpose of selling franchises.

The franchisor will also be developing the necessary information and skills in order to enable him to give advice to the franchisee in connection with the leasing of premises and other contracts into which the franchisee may have to enter with suppliers and with those who provide maintenance services generally in or about the conduct of the franchise business. The franchisor will also no doubt have made arrangements with sources of finance so that assistance can be given to franchisees who require loans or hire purchase for the purpose of financing the acquisition, the initial equipment package, and for paying for any of the necessary shopfitting and equipping work that is also required for the franchisee to open his business.

The franchisor will have to set up his selling organisation and, indeed, commence the development of his head office organisation. He will have to train the staff who are to be employed by the head office organisation. He will no doubt employ the nucleus of his team in the initial exploratory pilot operations. The franchisor's head office will ultimately have to be organised so as to cope with all the aspects that will arise. It will require specialists in the design and decor of the stores; in merchandising, in site selection; in product control and innovation; in equipment control and innovation; in accounting procedures and methods of business management; in advertising; in research of the future development and innovations to be incorporated into the franchise scheme.

Quite naturally in the early stages the organisation will not be very large as the business would not justify the expenditure at that stage. Indeed, a very small band of highly competent people will have to double up on many of these activities training others and hiving off their activities as the organisation grows. It is frequently the case in the early days of the development of a franchise company or even later in its development when it is growing at a very fast pace that it never really has enough head office staff to provide the sort of back-up service that is really essential. In these circumstances the franchisor and his staff are working very extensive hours. The timing of the development programme of the franchise is critical if one is to avoid the danger of going so fast that one is unable to provide the necessary services to those who are opening new franchises while at the same time providing the promised services on a continuing basis to those who have already been established in business.

The final matter which would have to be dealt with is, of course, the preparation of the legal documents which are necessary to ensure that the arrangements between the franchisor and franchisee are properly recorded in clear and unambiguous terms. The most important feature of these contracts is not the small print nor, indeed, the strict letter of the contract but that they should contain precisely what benefits the franchisee is going to receive and precisely what controls he can expect to have imposed upon him and his fellows.

No amount of print in a contract will satisfy a disgruntled franchisee who feels he has been sold something that did not represent what he was offered. The franchisor must be absolutely certain that he provides for his franchisee what he has told him he will provide. The quickest way to ensure the failure of a franchise operation is to have to explain to each franchisee when he complains that while he may have understood from the earlier discussions that something was agreed, if he would care to look at his contract he will see that there is no mention of it. A franchisor should bear in mind that at this stage he is laying the foundations and setting the tone for the future. If the foundations that are laid are not properly prepared he cannot expect the business that follows to be one that can be safely built upon.

CHAPTER 6

How the Franchisor Obtains His Income

CLEARLY the franchisor expects to receive payment for the package that he is selling to the franchisee and for the continuing service he will be providing to the franchisee.

The franchisor, when setting up his franchise scheme, will have to decide how much he requires by way of franchise fees in order to finance the provision of his services, give him a good return on his capital, and show a reasonable profit. The franchisee, on the other hand, wants to know how much money will be taken out of his business by the franchisor. While in practice there is little the franchisee can do to negotiate a franchisee fee, he must ascertain the sources of the franchisor's income. He must know the manner in which the franchise fees are to be calculated so that he can judge that the franchisor's fees are fair to both parties. The franchisor's approach to franchise fees, their extent and method of calculation, can also provide an interesting insight into the nature and attitudes of the franchisor. There are a number of different ways in which a franchise fee may be charged, and it is possible that franchise fees will be payable in more than one of the ways described.

The various methods by which a franchise fee is taken are as follows.

1. An Initial Franchise Fee

In some franchise schemes an initial franchise fee is payable on the signing of the franchise contract or on opening for business. In some cases, where the fee is sizeable, payment by instalments will be allowed.

It would be very unusual for this to be the only fee the franchisor will ever receive otherwise he would have no capacity to finance the continuing relationship. While such a fee is often taken it is invariably tied to one or other of the fees that are described below.

2. Sale of Initial Franchise Package

Many franchise schemes involve the purchase by the franchisee of a franchise package. This package will comprise a number of different elements, the sum total of which will equip the franchisee with the form of training pre-opening services supplies and equipment to enable the franchisee to be ready to open for business. The equipment and supplies element of the package will have been gathered together by the franchisor from various suppliers no doubt at a discount below the normal retail price. The franchisor will mark up the items included in the package to show himself a profit to cover the cost of getting the package together and for getting the franchisee into business. This mark up would contain a sufficient margin to allow for a contribution from this particular package sale to the general costs of running the franchisor's head office organisation.

3. Sale of Equipment

(a) Invariably there will be a sale of equipment included in the initial package as is mentioned above. What one must guard against, as a franchisee, is the possibility that what is being sold as a franchise is in effect a disguised sale of equipment. This is not necessarily wrong but it must be recognised for what it is. It will often be linked with an obligation to purchase from the seller (franchisor) material to be used with the equipment. Having established the correct nature of the transaction it can be placed into perspective and be properly assessed.

(b) In some cases there may be an obligation imposed upon the franchisee to purchase future supplies of novel or essential equipment from the franchisor. Such sale will undoubtedly include a profit element for the franchisor. In a franchise which is dependent upon a specialised piece of equipment the obligation may extend to the purchase and use of later and improved versions of the equipment. In such a case the franchisee should be satisfied that new equipment cannot be imposed ıpon him when the existing item of equipment is doing the job perfectly well, whatever the refinements the newer equipment may have.

4. Leasing of Premises

(a) Sometimes the franchisor will be able to negotiate terms for leasing a suitable site at extremely good terms in view of the covenant which the franchisor is able to offer the landlord. The franchisor may decide to sub-let these premises to the franchisee at a higher rent, thus showing a profit rental for himself.

(b) The franchisor may in some cases own the freehold of the premises from which the franchisee is to trade and will grant a lease to the franchisee. In both cases the franchisee should take care to ensure that the terms contained in the lease are those which obtain in the market. Care must also be taken to ensure that the franchisor does not use the lease to impose unreasonable conditions that he would not feel able to insert into the franchise contract.

5. Financing Arrangements

The franchisor may make arrangements with a finance company for a commission to be paid to him on the introduction of franchisees to the finance company. The franchisor may also set up his own finance company and make a profit on financing his own business.

6. Leasing of Equipment

Some franchisors arrange for the leasing of equipment to the franchisee rather than a sale so as to reduce the cost of the initial package. The franchisor may receive a commission from the finance company. Alternatively, but less frequently, the franchisor will lease the equipment direct to the franchisee and take his profit on that transaction.

7. Continuing Fees

(a) *Royalty payments.* The franchisor may charge a straight royalty on the gross sales of the franchisee. This may involve a minimum fee. There are some who consider that this is the best way as the franchisee knows precisely how much he has to pay up; he knows precisely how to calculate it and he knows that the franchisor will not be taking fees in any other way. The other view held by many is that this is not a good way to charge a franchise fee. The view is that psychologically the franchisee will not like parting with his money to somebody else. It can be painful parting with a slice of hard-earned cash. Further, as the franchisee feels a degree of independence of the franchisor which is a feeling which many successful franchisees do develop, he will become more reluctant to pay the franchise fee and more aware of the drain from his pocket.

There are many good franchises which operate on the royalty basis and there are many good franchises which operate on a different basis. Certainly, from the franchisor's point of view, it is a safe and reliable method. In the U.S.A., with its much more stringent anti-trust laws and other laws affecting franchising, the royalty method seems to be much the better system. One is inclined to the view that it is also in the long term the best method to employ in the U.K.

(b) *Sale of products.* In some franchises the agreement compels the franchisee to buy goods from the franchisor or a nominated supplier of the franchisor. The franchisor obtains his fee by marking up the goods so that he receives in fact a franchise royalty by taking a larger gross profit for the goods than he would otherwise have obtained. Where a nominated supplier is used the franchisor can obtain income by receiving a commission from the supplier.

One of the difficulties that can arise with this method of charging a franchise fee is that the franchisee can be at the mercy of an unscrupulous franchisor. There are undoubtedly very many companies which operate this sytem fairly and properly, often delaying price increases to the last possible moment. It is, nevertheless, a method of payment of a franchise fee which should be carefully scrutinised by the franchisee. The franchisee should satisfy himself that the franchisor is not taking advantage of him and that there are forms of protection upon which he can rely.

Two factors clearly emerge from the above; firstly, so far as the franchisor is concerned he must make a policy decision at the very earliest moment on the manner in which he will take his franchise fees. He must budget to ensure that the flow of fees that he receives from the various sources are sufficient to show him the return that he needs to cover his overheads and to make a reasonable profit. Secondly, so far as the franchisee is concerned he must ascertain the sources of the franchisor's income. He must satisfy himself that the franchisor will not be in a position unfairly to take advantage of him.

CHAPTER 7

The Franchisor's Initial Services to the Franchisee

THE following services will have to be provided by a franchisor to a franchisee before the franchisee is in a position to open for business. It is difficult to place these items in order of importance as most of them are equally important but in different ways.

There are, however, some that are very basic and one absolutely fundamental service which should be provided by a franchisor is training. Training will cover two aspects of the business.

Firstly, there is the basic business training which has to be given to the franchisee. This will include training in book-keeping skills, staff selection, staff management, business procedures and documentary systems necessary for the purposes of controlling the operation, and elementary business training which will enable the franchisee to do basic trouble shooting of his own. It should not be thought that this training will be so detailed that the franchisor will in effect be running a small business management college. The training will be limited in its application to giving to the franchisee the basic skills that are necessary for the purpose of the particular operation with which he is concerned.

The book-keeping system which will have been set up will have been so arranged as to provide the minimum of work and effort for the franchisee but the maximum of vital information. It will be geared to produce without too much difficulty the vital flow of financial management information which is necessary for the franchisee to see where he stands at all times. The value of up-to-date meaningful financial information cannot be emphasised too much. It should show trends and strains which if correctly interpreted should enable appropriate action to be taken in relation to the business at the latest possible moment.

The staff selection and staff management training the franchisee will receive will give him the basic skills that he requires for interviewing staff, assessing their capabilities, and training them in the work which they have to do. Handling people is largely a matter of experience, but there are nevertheless guidelines which can be given to help the inexperienced. The franchisee will, when he allies practical experience to the principles which have been laid down for him, find that he is achieving far more than he would otherwise have been capable of.

The franchisor may prepare certain forms which the franchisee will have to complete. These forms will be designed to show the performance of the operation and demonstrate to franchisor and franchisee the areas in which the franchisee needs to improve his performance. There should be a sound reason for any documents which the franchisee is compelled by the franchisor to complete. It is not the franchisee's function merely to operate as a source of useless information.

The franchisee should be trained so that he is able to detect problems as they arise in his business and thus be in a position to take remedial action without waiting for the franchisor's trouble shooters to call upon him and diagnosing that trouble is brewing.

The training that will be given to the franchisee will not be as wide ranging and thorough as it would have to be if he were being prepared to cope with the unknown; he is only prepared to cope with the business which is being franchised to him. His training will therefore be limited in this way.

The second area in which training will be given to the franchisee relates to the operational details of the business.

In a food franchise, for example, the franchisee will be taught portion control, quality control, preparation methods, any particular recipes, and any particular processes which will have to be applied to the food before it is passed on to the consumer.

The franchisee may be required to attend a special training school to be trained in these aspects. Above all one thing must occur, whether or not there is a training school, and that is that the franchisee must after he completes his training be capable of stepping into his own business and opening and running it without pausing to scratch his head and wonder where his next piece of inspiration will come from.

Apart from these areas of training the franchisor should perform other functions.

The franchisor will, with the criteria for site selection that he has established, investigate and evaluate sites for the franchisee. He will advise whether or not the sites come within his accepted standards and what sort of performance can be expected of them. This is a very critical area of the franchisor's functions. One franchise company has instructed its site finders that unless the site that they are viewing is one into which they would invest every last penny that they possess they would not approve it for the purpose of a franchisee's business. This may sound drastic but is certainly a sound principle upon which to operate. No franchisor should expect a franchisee to invest his money in something in which the franchisor would not himself invest. The franchisee should appreciate that in approving a site a franchisor is not infallible and that he cannot guarantee that his judgement is correct. For the franchisee blindly to accept the franchisor's opinion without question can be dangerous. The franchisee should closely question the franchisor, particularly if he has doubts about the site himself.

Having selected a site the franchisor should give assistance to the franchisee in obtaining any necessary consents under the Town and Country Planning legislation and the local building by-laws.

He should also assist the franchisee in the design and remodelling of the store, assist him with the shopfitting, and in many cases prepare and submit plans for the shopfitters to work from. The franchisor will in many instances give the franchisee assistance in deciding which particular shopfitter's estimates to accept. The franchisor may also give the franchisee assistance in the supervision of the shopfitters while they carry out their work. Most franchisors, although they offer such assistance, will not be prepared to accept the responsibility which the franchisee's own surveyor would, for example, accept. Specialised professional advice is the responsibility of the franchisee.

The franchisor will, if standardised equipment is not already part of the package which he has sold to the franchisee, give advice and assistance in selection of the correct equipment at the most economic prices. He should have all the relevant information readily available.

A further service which many franchisors offer to franchisees is assistance in negotiating a lease of the premises with the landlords or their agents and assisting the franchisee in completing his arrangements with the benefit of expert and experienced help.

Part of the training which the franchisee will have received will have included some guidance on marketing and promotional principles, and the franchisor should suppy to the franchisee initial quantities of marketing and promotional material, point of sale advertising, and the like.

The franchisor will provide for the franchisee a statement setting out the amount of the opening stock inventory which he should hold and will make arrangements for the franchisee to purchase these stocks from his own purchasing department or from suppliers who are nominated for the purpose. It is important that the franchisor should give to the franchisee a realistic breakdown of his cash requirements. In particular the franchisee must be able to ascertain what proportion of his investment is required to purchase the franchise package and what proportion is being set aside for working capital. Proper provision must be made for working capital in the calculations of the franchisee's cash requirements. If the franchisor's projections do not take this into account they must be viewed with some degree of care and the franchisor closely questioned about the matter. Any calculations or projections which do not allow for working capital are bound to be unrealistic, and raise a large question mark about the validity of the franchisor's other statements or representations about the franchise scheme.

The franchisor should provide for the franchisee on the spot assistance in the final arrangements before the store opens for business and in getting the business open.

The franchisor will frequently provide opening assistance by having a team of as many as two or three people present to assist the franchisee in getting the business off the ground. Initially they may have to cope with a rush of business as the public try out the business. The franchisor's opening crew will seek to ensure that the franchisee is properly putting into practice the principles which have been instilled in him during training. The opening crew should stay on the premises until they are satisfied that the franchisee has got into the swing of things and is coping well enough to be left on his own.

It is only when he is left alone after the initial shock that the franchisee will really come into his own and begin to develop his true potential. At this stage, it is important to emphasise again that the franchisee must realise that no franchisor can guarantee to him success, least of all success without work. A franchise is not a passage to wealth without effort. Most franchises will require long hours of solid work on the part of the franchisee in order to achieve success. What the franchisor is offering is a ready-made formula for carrying on business which in similar circumstances has proved to be successful. He will give to the franchisee whatever assistance he can in an endeavour to ensure that the franchisee will achieve a similar degree of success. This cannot be guaranteed, and any franchisor who offers firm guarantees of success to franchisees should be viewed with caution.

CHAPTER 8

The Continuing Services and Franchise Relationship

ONCE the franchisee has opened for business the most obvious help that he will require from the franchisor is the regular visit of the franchisor's field man, the trouble shooter. Regular visits should take place, and the trouble shooter should be available at short notice if the franchisee feels that he has a problem.

The trouble shooter may find on a regular routine visit to the franchisee's business that all is not well and that certain retraining is necessary. In such a case he will then stay with the business and on the premises while he retrains the franchisee and puts him on the right lines. The franchisee must not rely too heavily on the trouble shooter; he must learn to solve his own problems; he should look to the franchisor merely as a shoulder to lean upon and as a source of assistance to him when things get a bit too much. The franchisor's trouble shooter should also be available at all times to the franchisee when required. The words "when required" are used advisedly. The franchisor cannot be expected to know by some telepathic process that the franchisee expects help from him at any particular time. Communication is an essential feature of the relationship. The franchisee must keep in touch with the franchisor and must let the franchisor know when he does have difficulties. The franchisee must not delude himself, he must face up to difficulties as they arise and not try to pretend they do not exist.

The franchisee should phone the trouble shooter from time to time if he has not been visited and have a chat with him, for out of these discussions much good can come. He must also read very carefully all literature and circulars that reach him through the franchisor, for by this means if the franchisor is performing his functions correctly the franchisee will be supplied with a lot of information. Nothing could be more annoying to the trouble shooter, or indeed to the franchisee, for the franchisee to call in assistance when the answer to the problems that he has are contained in the literature that has been circulated to him but he just has not bothered to read it.

The franchisee must appreciate that the trouble shooter wants to work with him to help him but that he must help himself. He cannot expect the franchisor to run his business for him. The franchisee must mentally adjust to the fact that he is a businessman in his own right and behave as one.

The franchisor will through the trouble shooter and through regularly called meetings and seminars keep in touch with the franchisee and initiate such retraining processes as are necessary. It may well be that some new equipment or some new line will emerge with which the franchisee has to cope. The franchisor will then have to train the franchisee so that he is able to cope with the innovation.

While on the subject of innovation, of course, the franchisor will have research facilities in relation to the product, the format, and the market image that it is projecting of its business. He will be constantly seeking to innovate and introduce ideas and methods for improving the business of the franchised chain.

The franchisor will seek to keep the franchisees in touch with each other and with each other's success and problems. The franchisor will often run a journal for this purpose. The journal will publicise to the franchisees the successes that are being achieved, set targets for them, and provide an interchange of ideas. Successful schemes which franchisees have evolved for their own benefit are in this way also made available for the benefit of all franchisees within the chain. Much can be done through the imaginative use of journals of this nature to introduce a competitive element among the franchisees and a corporate pride in the activities of the whole chain.

The franchisor will run national and local advertising schemes and also ensure that the important field of public relations is looked after. The advertising schemes will be calculated to exploit to the full the national corporate image of a chain providing services in many areas and to capitalise on the strong features of the franchise.

The cost of advertising will be dealt with in one of two ways. It may be borne by the franchisor out of his franchise fee income. In this case the franchise fee will allow a margin for such expenditure. Alternatively, it may be charged to the franchisee as a separate item. If it is so charged the normal arrangement is for the advertising contribution to be paid into a separate account and the funds strictly accounted for.

The franchisor will seek to exploit the franchise utilising market research as an aid to discover those areas in which the appeal is strongest. Throughout, the franchisor must be very market conscious and must be prepared to exploit the opportunities that arise.

Indeed, the franchisor must seek to create opportunity where none appeared to exist. To this end the franchisor should be seeking to exploit new sources of supply of good quality materials, supplies, or products for the franchisees so that their costs are kept to the most economic levels possible. As the chain grows the bulk purchasing power of the whole group will also grow, resulting in a considerable account with a manufacturer or supplier. This should produce valuable savings for each individual franchisee. Benefits and savings can thus be effected for franchisees which would not be available to them with only their own resources to bring into play.

In the background of all this activity there is, of course, the head office organisation of the franchisor. The organisation that should contain specialists in each of the fields in which the franchisee is likely to require assistance. There should be specialists in the management and book-keeping aspects of the business; there should be specialists in advertising marketing public relations; specialists in product quality and control, equipment quality and control; specialists in all the various aspects of the business with which the franchised chain is concerned. There is also the franchisor's field force operating directly with the franchisees, including the trouble shooter.

In these circumstances the franchisee is better off than the manager of a local branch within a national chain. In a national chain the accent will be on ensuring that the manager runs his branch in accordance with the policy of the company. While to some extent this would apply to a franchised organisation, there is not the same rigidity. Each franchisee is treated as an individual. His problems are treated as those of an individual, and the approach of the team at the highest management level is not to dictate to the franchisee what he should do and what company policy is, but to try and train him and to instil in him the interest which an individual should have in running and managing his own business.

The franchisor's interest is in seeking to achieve for the franchisee the success of which his business is capable and in bringing the best out of him as an individual. The franchisor should certainly not dictate to the franchisee.

The franchisor may also be a source for the franchisee to obtain a prospective purchaser for his business. Whether things are going well or not it is quite likely that the franchisor will have contact with many people interested in taking over a business of this sort. The franchisee can often obtain valuable assistance from a franchisor when he does decide for some reason or other that the time has come to dispose of his business.

The clear lesson is that the important factors for success in this stage are good communications, co-operation between the franchisor and franchisee, and a clear understanding of the relationship that exists between them.

CHAPTER 9

The Franchise Contract

THE franchise contract is a very important document. It is the moment of truth. It is the occasion when the franchisor's promises have to be presented to the franchisee in writing and be subjected to careful scrutiny.

The contract is a legal commitment which is binding on both parties. The franchisee must therefore at this stage take competent legal advice as to the meaning and effect of the contract. In consultation with his solicitor he will check to see whether the contract confirms what he has been told. The franchisee should realise that the extent of the advice he is given is limited to the meaning and effect of the contract. It is the decision of the franchisee and the franchisee alone whether or not to proceed with any particular franchise opportunity. Decision making is an essential part of his role as a businessman.

A franchise contract has to take into account a number of different considerations. The essential considerations may be considered under nine separate headings.

1. Although basically a contractual relationship between the franchisor and the franchisee, the franchise contract involves two other parties who are not joined as parties to the contract. The other parties are, firstly, all other franchisees within the franchise chain and, secondly, members of the public, the consumer, and it is to both of these parties that the franchisor and the franchisee owe considerable responsibilities. It is simple to see how this arises. Each franchisee within the chain will be affected for good or bad by the actions of his fellow franchisees. If a franchisee runs his operation in a manner which is inconsistent with the standards associated with the franchisor's brand name and image, it will damage the goodwill associated with them, thereby adversely affecting the business prospects of other franchisees. So each franchisee owes a

heavy responsibility to the other franchisees and should therefore look on the restrictive provisions of the agreement which are concerned with the maintenance of the standards and the correct operation of the franchised business as not merely a tiresome chore but as a duty and responsibility which he owes to himself and his fellow franchisees to ensure that the reputation and status of the franchise chain is always maintained.

The consumer features in this, of course, because the consumer is not concerned with whether or not an outlet is franchised. A consumer is merely concerned with the brand image. A consumer will frequent a business which has given satisfaction in the past and will regard franchised businesses as being branches of a larger chain. He will not accept an explanation "but this was operated under franchise and unfortunately we have problems with that franchisee" if the franchisee does not do his job properly. All the consumer is concerned with is that when he goes into the store he receives the same standards of products and service that he has been led to believe he can expect from that particular "branded" business.

Franchisees therefore owe a great responsibility in the maintenance of these standards to ensure that the consumer is not misled and that whichever outlet within the franchise chain the consumer patronises he feels that he is being given the sort of product and service he had reason to expect he would receive.

2. It has already been explained that the franchisor in a business format franchise will be contributing his blue print which embraces a package comprising trade secrets, method of operation, use of trade marks, trade names, and many of the other features previously mentioned. The franchisor will be concerned in his agreement to ensure that provision is made for the franchisee (a) to use these blue prints, methods of operation, trade marks, trade names, etc., and (b) to preserve the element of trade secrecy which is associated with the franchisor's particular methods and blue prints.

3. In order to achieve the goal it is inherent in discharging the fourway obligations outlined in item 1 above that consideration is given to the manner in which the necessary standards are imposed upon the franchisee and what provision should be made to enforce those standards.

4. It will also be advisable that over the passage of years the freshness of the image and appeal to the consumer is maintained, and it will therefore

be a concern to ensure that provision is made and means are available to require the franchisee to make provision for, by setting amounts aside periodically, investment in the modernisation and the up-grading of the premises and equipment employed therein so that with the passage of time the appeal of the business and its attractiveness to the consumer does not fade.

5. Another consideration is the method by which the franchisor obtains his income.

6. Consideration will have to be given to the question of the circumstances in which the franchise arrangement can be terminated. In doing so, the position of the franchisee must be considered responsibly so that the franchise cannot be terminated capriciously. Consequences of termination also have to be clearly thought out.

7. It is also a prime consideration and in practice an area of great difficulty in making provision in the agreement for the circumstances in which an assignment might take place. Obviously in a franchise which requires the franchisee to be trained, as most do, or which may require a specialised area of knowledge or the application of particular principles a franchisee can never be permitted freely to assign his franchise when disposing of his business. Safeguards have to be built in to ensure that the new franchisee will accept the responsibilities, will undergo any necessary training, and have the ability to perform the obligations in the agreement so as to maintain the same standards of service and product as if, in fact, there had been no change of franchisee.

8. Another area to which considerable thought has to be given is what is to happen if the franchisee, being an individual, or if the principal shareholder and director of the franchisee, if it is a limited company, dies. Some franchise agreements make no provisions at all for these circumstances, others do make certain provisions. Clearly, it is an area of serious concern for both franchisor and franchisee that the right balance is struck so that the dependants of the franchisee are able either to continue the business formerly carried on by the deceased or, alternatively, are able to turn the business to account by selling and receiving the capital value of the business.

9. The agreement must also be considered from the franchisee's point of view. Quite apart from the consideration that is given to the franchisee's point of view in the aspects already dealt with, the franchisee must satisfy

himself that the contract offers him exactly what he has been led to believe he would receive. He should not leave anything to trust; he should ask the franchisor to write into the agreement, or perhaps as an amendment to the agreement, confirmation of all the obligations undertaken. Nothing should be left to implication.

Furthermore, although the tendency exists for a successful franchisee to forget what he owes to the franchisor for his success, the franchisor will invariably always know just that little bit more about the business than any one individual franchisee. In such a case the franchisor must be able to contain the franchisee within the scope of the franchise scheme.

It will be appreciated that not all the provisions referred to in this chapter will apply in every case, but some, indeed most, will feature in all franchise transactions.

A franchise transaction conveniently splits into two stages:

Stage one is that which exists prior to the opening of the business.
Stage two is that which exists after the business is open.

Some franchise companies accordingly have two contracts, one for each stage. In such cases the stage one contract is frequently called a purchase agreement and the stage two contract the franchise or licence agreement. Let us examine each in turn.

The purchase agreement may be conveniently divided into three aspects:

1. The franchise package.
2. The price.
3. The services to be provided.

Before examining each of these aspects it should be noted that it is not essential that the premises from which the franchisee is to trade should be finally agreed upon before the contracts are signed. As long as it is possible to pinpoint an area within which the premises are to be located, the agreements may be made conditionally upon a mutually acceptable site being found. This may appear at first sight to be potentially dangerous, but a successful franchise will usually attract more franchisees than can be placed at any given time. A waiting list will develop. In such a case prospective franchisees will wish to join the queue and reserve an area, indeed it is possible in some cases to obtain an option from a franchisor for an area.

A purchase agreement will specify the site or an area within which the premises are to be located.

1. The Franchise Package

The extent and subject matter of the franchise package that is being sold will be listed. The list is sometimes called an inventory of equipment or perhaps just an equipment list. It must contain all items that are included; all items that the franchisee has been told to expect. Some franchise companies regard this list as being confidential and stipulate in the contract that it must be so treated by the franchisee. In such a case there will also be a provision requiring the return of the list if the transaction does not proceed.

2. The Price

The price will be specified, as will be the manner of payment. This may be cash in full on signature, although this is rare. More often a deposit is required on signature with payment of the balance to follow on delivery of the equipment.

There may be allowance for the fact that finance has to be arranged. In this case the contract may be conditional upon satisfactory finance being obtained. What is to be regarded as "satisfactory finance" should be carefully defined.

The price may not include delivery charges, installation charges, shopfitting work and VAT. If this is the case it should be made clear particularly in respect of the shopfitting work. This latter can often cause confusion as the equipment list will often include equipment and fittings which will be incorporated in the shopfitting.

If a deposit is paid at this stage is should be made clear whether and in what circumstances it is returnable to the franchisee. The franchisor will wish at this stage to retain the right to withdraw from the transaction. It may be that training will show the franchisee to be unsuitable for the particular type of franchise. In a case where the franchisor withdraws from the transaction the deposit should be returnable to the franchisee in full. However, a different situation obtains if the franchisee wishes to withdraw. The franchisor may be prepared to take a risk on his own withdrawal, but if the franchisee can withdraw without cost after having caused the franchisor a lot of trouble and expense, then the payment of the deposit will not amount to much evidence of good faith. Provision is therefore usually made for the franchisor to be able to retain part of the deposit to reimburse to him the expenses in which he has been involved.

3. The Services To Be Provided

These services to the franchisee will be set out. They have been discussed in some detail in Chapter 7.

These are the main features to be expected in a purchase agreement. If in a particular transaction there is no purchase agreement then such of these features as are relevant to the transaction should be found in the franchise or licence agreement.

The franchise or licence agreement can be conveniently divided into six sections:

Section 1. The rights granted to the franchisee.
Section 2. The obligations undertaken by the franchisor.
Section 3. The obligations imposed by the franchisee.
Section 4. The trading restrictions imposed upon the franchisee.
Section 5. Assignment/death of franchisee.
Section 6. The termination provisions.

Section 1

The franchisee will be given the right so far as may be relevant in the particular circumstances:

(a) To use the trade marks and patents of the franchisor.
(b) To use the brand image and the design and decor of the premises developed by the franchisor in projecting that image.
(c) To use the franchisor's secret methods.

(d) To use the recipes, formulae, specifications, and processes and methods of manufacture developed by the franchisor.

(e) To conduct the franchised business upon or from the agreed premises strictly in accordance with the franchisor's methods and subject to the franchisor's directions.

It should be noted that many franchise schemes carry with them the promise of exclusive rights. These exclusive rights will vary according to whether the franchised business is physically immobile, e.g. a retail shop, or physically mobile, e.g. an ice-cream van. In the case of a retail shop the exclusivity would be based upon a radius within which the franchisor will not franchise another similar unit. In the case of a mobile franchise an area within which the franchisee may carry on his business will be exclusively granted and the franchisee will be forbidden to step outside such area.

It is difficult to lay down any set radius, for what is reasonable will vary considerably from case to case. It is important to realise that the franchisor cannot hope for a successful healthy growth in his own business if his units are placed so close together that none can effectively operate.

An additional factor that must be taken into account in approaching the problem of exclusivity of area is the growing legislative (both domestic and European) intervention. This intervention is sought to be politically justified on the basis that the legislation will curb abuse of monopoly power and encourage the free development of the markets. Franchising is likely to be affected by any such legislation although one is inclined to doubt that the arguments justifiably apply to franchising.

(f) The right to obtain supplies from nominated suppliers at special prices. The franchisor can often obtain quite good reductions for franchisees using the weight of the bulk-purchasing powers of the whole of the franchised chain.

In some cases the franchisor requires the franchisee to purchase his supplies of products or raw materials from the franchisor. This is often the case where a trade mark is involved and is, for example, a feature of the Wimpy franchise. This type of provision is also likely to attract the same sort of legislative attention to which reference has already been made in relation to exclusivity of territory.

Section 2

The obligations of the franchisor in the continuing relationship that exists after the business has opened are dealt with in Chapter 8.

Section 3

The franchisee may have the obligation imposed upon him:

(a) To carry on the business franchised and no other upon the premises and strictly in accordance with the franchisor's methods and standards. This provision will often be detailed enough to prevent the sale of any items not included in the franchise scheme unless the franchisor expressly gives his consent. In some cases even automatic vending machines and juke boxes are expressly prohibited to maintain the standards and appearance of the operation.

(b) To observe certain minimum opening hours. These will usually be the hours that enable the business to be operated most profitably within the scope of the blue prints and without incurring disproportionate overheads. For example, the cost of staff and other overheads in remaining open for, say, a further two hours a day may not be covered by the additional trading that is done.

(c) To pay a franchise fee. The various methods by which a franchisor receives payment of such a fee are dealt with in detail in Chapter 6.

(d) To follow the accounting system laid down by the franchisor. The purpose is twofold. Firstly, the franchisor has a means of checking and for the purpose of calculating any fees to which he may be entitled. Secondly, the system will be prepared in such a way that it will rapidly reveal if the projected gross and net profit margins are being maintained. Any differences that are thus revealed can be quickly investigated and the appropriate remedial action taken.

(e) Not to advertise without prior approval of the advertisements by the franchisor. As has been explained, the franchisor will invariably handle all national advertising but this will not mean that there is no local or other advertising that cannot benefit the business. The franchisor will wish to have control of the contents of advertisements that make use of his name and relate to one of his franchised businesses.

(f) To use and display such point of sale or advertising material as the franchisor stipulates. Also to use bags, boxes, wrappers, and, in a food franchise, even such items as straws, cups, and serviettes bearing the franchisor's name and trade mark. Point of sale and advertising material is often supplied free of charge, but the other items would, of course, have to be paid for.

(g) To maintain the premises in a good, clean sanitary condition and to redecorate when required to do so by the franchisor. This is a provision that often causes difficulty. The franchisor will always be striving to ensure that the premises have the best possible appearance while the franchisee will be reluctant to spend his money.

(h) To maintain the widest possible business insurance cover. The purpose of this provision is to protect the franchisee from the consequences of fire or public or employees' liability and other claims. It protects his business and his livelihood.

(i) To permit the franchisor's staff to enter the premises to inspect and see whether the franchisor's standards are being maintained and whether the terms of the agreement are being observed.

(j) To purchase a minimum quantity of goods or products from the franchisor or his nominated suppliers. This provision would apply in a case where the franchisor manufactures some or all of the products that are to be sold in the franchised business.

(k) To train his staff in the franchisor's methods and to ensure that they are neatly and appropriately clothed.

(l) Not to assign the franchise contract without the franchisor's consent, such consent not to be unreasonably withheld. All franchise contracts should be capable of assignment. If the contract is not assignable there is no incentive to the franchisee to invest and to build. The franchisor, however, will have controls over the acceptance of franchisees and will not wish to have the controls avoided. There is rarely difficulty in practice in arranging a transfer of the franchise provided the incoming person matches the franchisor's selection standards and passes through any necessary training.

Section 4

The restrictions imposed upon the franchisee may prohibit him from:

(a) Carrying on a similar business except under franchise from the franchisor. The franchisor will not wish to train the franchisee only to have him open a similar business trading in competition with the other franchisees without regard to the territorial restrictions.

(b) Taking staff away from other franchisees. As all franchisees are dependent upon each other it would not be in the interests of the development of the chain for franchisees to be attempting to take trained staff away from each other.

(c) Carrying on a similar business in close proximity to the other franchised businesses within the chain for a certain period after the termination of the franchise contract. This provision is to protect all the franchisees within the chain.

(d) Continuing after the termination of the franchise contract to use any of the franchisor's trade names, trade secrets, secret processes, recipes, specifications, and the like.

Section 5

The question of assignability has been mentioned in the comments in Section 3. The problem of what should be done in the event of the death of the franchisee or the principal shareholder of the franchisee if it is a company has not been faced up to by many franchise contracts. The franchisee should ensure that in the event of death:

(a) His personal representative and/or dependants can keep the business going until one of them can qualify as a franchisee and take an assignment of the franchise agreement; or

(b) That arrangement can be made to keep the business going until a suitable assignee can be found at a proper price. In this respect the franchisor may be able to agree to offer to provide management (for a fee) during the critical few weeks following the death. All reputable and ethical franchisors will be sympathetic and helpful whatever the contract provides, but it is best if the contract clearly specifies what will happen.

Section 6

The agreement may be determinable after the expiration of the fixed period or there may be express provision for termination upon the service of a notice. Inevitably the agreement will provide for determination by the franchisor in the event of any default by the franchisee of his obligations under the franchise agreement. Most agreements provide a machinery for the franchisee to be given an opportunity to remedy any defaults which can be remedied within a specified period before the franchisor can exercise the right of determination.

In whatever circumstances the franchise agreement is determined the franchisee should be left with a business and the equipment for which he has paid. He will be stripped of this right to carry on business under the trade name and lose all the advantages available to a franchisee, but that is all.

In some cases the franchisor will own the freehold or lease of the premises and will grant a lease or an underlease to the franchisee. In such a case the franchisee may find that upon the termination of the franchise agreement he has lost his lease also. In such a case the franchisee should at the time of the signature of the contract see that there are safeguards for the cash investment he is making. In doing so he must appreciate that the basic cause for him subsequently finding himself in such an invidious position will be his own default.

In view of the close working relationship that must exist between a franchisor and a franchisee all requirements must be clearly stated in the contract. This is a transaction in which no small print should exist.

CHAPTER 10

The Choice of Franchise and What To Ask the Franchisor

A PERSON who decides to go into business on his own account has to make a number of decisions. These decisions will be about what type of business to go into, where it should be situated, what can be afforded, and so on.

A prospective franchisee is in the same position except that his basic decision is which franchisor and which franchise scheme to select.

A prospective franchisee must obtain advice from others who are able to view the matter objectively and reliably. This would include his wife, whose support is essential, his solicitors, his accountant, and his friends already in business. It is also helpful to consult with any outside agencies such as trade organisations who may be able to give guidance on trends in a particular type of business.

The advice thus received must be balanced and weighed up by the franchisee and the factors relevant to the particular franchise considered. The final judgement and decision rests with the franchisee.

In choosing a franchise it is important that the franchisee should feel happy and at home with the business. He must feel certain that it is the right business for him and the right business for him to be involved in. Previous experience is not needed for taking up a franchise. The franchisor's training programme and continuing guidance should render this unnecessary. Indeed time and again franchisors find that those without previous experience or preconceived notions are better than those who have such experience. The latter are apt to consider that their ideas are best and that the franchisor does not know what should really be done. This is, of course, an attitude that can lead to a conflict in a relationship which must be harmonious. Those without experience are content to be guided.

There are some who will have a preference for working with their hands and they will tend towards a franchise which involves such work. Others, perhaps with engaging personalities, who enjoy meeting people, may prefer a franchise involving salesmanship or direct contact with the consumer. Aptitude and inclination is very much a factor affecting a franchisee's choice of franchise.

Apart from the selection of the type of franchise the franchisee has to make a decision on two other aspects of the transaction:

1. Is this the franchisor for me?
2. How does the franchise stand up under inquiry?

To investigate these aspects the following questions should be put to the franchisor:

1. How long have you been in franchising?
2. How many franchised businesses are you running at the moment?
3. What are the addresses of these businesses?
4. May I please interview any number of these franchisees? May I choose whom I interview?
5. What does your head office organisation consist of?
6. Can you demonstrate your capacity to provide the necessary follow-up service?
7. May I take up your bank reference?
8. Are there any other referees whom I may approach?
9. How many business failures have been experienced by your franchisees?
10. On what basis do you choose your franchisees—how selective are you?
11. How much does your franchise cost?
    (a) What does this price include?
    (b) What capital costs will be incurred in addition to this price and what for?
    (c) Do I have to pay a deposit? If so, in what circumstances do I get it back or will you keep all or part of it?
12. How much working capital do I need?
13. What are the costs incurred in the business likely to be broken down into:

    (a) Gross profit.

(b) Net profit.
Do these figures take my salary and depreciation into account?

14. May I see actual accounts which confirm or fail to confirm your projections?
15. Did you run your own pilot schemes before franchising?
16. If not, why not?
17. Whether you did or not what is the extent of your own cash investment in the business?
18. What financing arrangements can you make and what terms for repayment will there be. What rate of interest will be required and will the finance company want security?
19. Is the business seasonal?
20. When is the best time to open up?
21. What fees do you charge?
22. Do you take any commission on supplies of goods or materials to a franchisee?
23. Will I be obliged to maintain a minimum fee or a minimum purchase of goods? What happens if I fail to meet this commitment?
24. What advertising and promotional expenditure do you incur?
25. Do I have to contribute to it, if so how much?
26. What initial services do you offer?
27. Do you train me? Who pays for my training? Where do I go for training?
28. What continuing services do you provide after the business has commenced?
29. May I have a copy of your franchise contracts?
30. Does this contract permit me to sell my business? What restrictions are there affecting my right to sell the business?
31. For how long is the franchise granted?
32. What happens at the end of that period?
33. What will happen if I do not like the business? Upon what basis can I terminate the contract?
34. Who will be my link with you after I have opened for business? Can I meet some of your staff?
35. What point of sale and promotional literature do you supply and what do I have to pay for it?

36. What will the opening hours of the business be?
37. Will I own all the equipment necessary to operate the business when I have cleared the finance company?
38. How soon will I have to spend money on redecorating the business?
39. How soon will I have to spend money on replacing equipment?
40. Will you find me a site or do I have to find it?
41. What systems do you have for keeping franchisees in touch with you and each other? Do you publish a newsletter? Do you hold seminars?
42. What help will I receive in local advertising and promotion?
43. What exclusive rights do I get?
44. How will I cope with my book-keeping?
45. What can I sell and what can I not sell?
46. Do you provide instruction and operational manuals?
47. What would happen if you misjudged the site and it did not produce the anticipated figures but resulted in a loss?
48. What would happen if I ran into operational problems I was not able to solve? What help would I get?
49. How can I be sure you will do what you promise?
50. Are you a member of the British Franchise Association, if not, why not?

All reputable franchisors will welcome these questions and indeed some of them will insist on certain steps, e.g., that the franchisee takes legal advice before signing. The franchisee should never be afraid to ask a question and should carefully note and weigh up the reply, making sure he has received a proper reply.

The recent formation of the British Franchise Association has introduced a new element. Membership is open only to those whose franchise scheme has been carefully scrutinised and who are prepared to accept and observe a strict code of ethical behaviour. In Appendix A there is set out an explanation of the aims, objectives, and practices of the Association so that the franchisee can judge the value of the franchisor having membership of the Association.

The franchisee should not rush his decision. He should take his time and have a good look round. The value of the answers received will be a matter for the franchisee's judgement. The franchisee can, of course, verify the value of the answer by the experience of existing franchisees. They are a very important factor to him in reaching a decision. They have been living with the business and with the franchisor for some time already. The franchisee must choose those whom he wishes to interview. He should not let the franchisor feed to him only his best franchisees.

Lastly, a franchisee should not let himself be weighed down by advice of others. He must put their advice and comments into perspective. It is after all the franchisee's money and life that will be affected by his decision.

CHAPTER 11

Franchising in Action—Eight Case Studies

TO DEMONSTRATE the application in practice of the principles that have been explained, the franchise propositions of the eight founder members of the British Franchise Association have been selected.

Budget Rent-a-Car (U.K.) Ltd.	Car hire
Dyno-Rod Ltd.	Drain cleaning and hygiene
Holiday Inns (U.K.) Inc.	Hotel
Kentucky Fried Chicken (G.B.) Ltd.	Fast food Kentucky fried chicken
Prontaprint Ltd.	Speedy print service
ServiceMaster Ltd.	On site cleaning and restoration service
Wimpy International Ltd.	Fast food Wimpy hamburgers
Ziebart Mobile Transport Service Ltd.	Car undersealing service

Each of these companies has prepared a presentation of its franchise proposition for this book.

These eight companies, as will be seen, operate in seven different fields ranging from the down to earth Dyno-Rod drain cleaning service to the international hotel chain, Holiday Inns. Whatever the difference between their areas of operation, each of them offers a franchise which embraces the features of the orthodox business format franchise.

In relation to the Dyno-Rod, ServiceMaster, and Wimpy franchises we have the additional benefit of the statistical information prepared by Dr. John Stanworth contained in Appendix B, which is referred to in the comments following each of these company's presentations.

It is interesting to note that some of the conclusions that Dr. Stanworth felt were indicated by his researches included:

(i) At least some of the franchisees felt that they would never have become self-employed but for the opportunity which franchising gave them.

(ii) Most franchisees felt that the public did not understand franchising and saw franchisees as employees of the company under whose trade name they operated.

(iii) Most franchisees felt that the quality of the training, equipment, supplies, and general back-up service given by the franchisor was good.

(iv) Nearly 90 per cent of the franchisees felt that franchising had enabled them to set up and develop their business more rapidly than would otherwise have been the case.

(v) Seventy per cent of the franchisees felt that a franchised business reduced the risk of failure.

(vi) Eighty per cent of the franchisees felt that their franchisor's trade mark was an important element in their success.

(vii) Eighty per cent of the franchisees did not consider any franchise other than the one they entered under.

(viii) Most franchisees experienced enough independence within the terms of the franchise contracts to feel they really were self employed.

(ix) Most franchisees said that their business had fulfilled their original ambitions and that they would recommend others to do as they had done.

Dr. Stanworth's research covered a wider field than that with which this work is concerned. The statistics extracted from his survey have been selected by the author solely on the basis of their relevance to the topics covered by this work. The whole of Appendix B including any comments are either extracted directly from the survey or was contributed by Dr. Stanworth.

Each Company's franchise proposition will be considered in turn.

Budget Rent-a-Car (U.K.) Ltd.

The Budget Rent-a-Car System is represented in more than thirty countries throughout the world and is recognised as one of the world's largest vehicle rental companies, with over

60,000 vehicles being rented from 1250 locations, more than 230 of them being situated within airport terminal buildings.

It is a subsidiary of the Transamerica Corporation of America which amongst others encompasses Trans-International Airlines, United Artists films, and Occidental Life Insurance. The U.K. and European head office is located in Hatfield, Hertfordshire.

In the field of vehicle rental the Budget licensee who will, generally, be running a compatible business such as a motor dealership, parking, travel, or hotel business has the following advantages:

  (i) He has a premise in the local market, although Budget will assist him in finding an appropriate site if he does not already possess one.

  (ii) He knows the people in his market and they know him.

  (iii) He is financially involved in the business and so has a direct interest in optimising the various factors of the business to produce a maximum profit.

  (iv) With Budget's advice and guidance he is in a position to own and service vehicles at the minimum cost per month.

  (v) His business has the opportunity to grow in size and profit when small businesses are going to the wall and large businesses find it very difficult to obtain profit orientated management.

Vehicle rental is a very specialised business which can either be highly profitable or disastrous depending upon the degree of attention and expertise applied to the business.

Budget Rent-a-Car (U.K.) Ltd. is in the position of being able to provide the vital expertise and know-how of the vehicle rental industry at a nominal cost compared to the cost to a licensee of providing the same expertise himself.

Budget Rent-a-Car provides the following benefits for its licensees:

1. Advertising and Promotion

Budget Rent-a-Car prides itself on its dynamic marketing and promotional approach which is directed at both the national business user and the local renter. A sum in excess of £250,000 per year is spent within the U.K. on such local and national advertising, promotional, and collateral back-up material.

New licensees receive considerable financial support for advertising and promotion activities in their local market during their first twelve months of operation.

2. Corp Rate

This is the name given to the programme which is aimed at the national business user. A team of national sales executives supported by research personnel are constantly selling to major accounts on behalf of the system. A complete range of billing systems has been devised which allows the Budget system to compete directly with other national car rental companies in the U.K. Over 1200 national companies are registered as regular users of Budget's services, amongst these are many of the largest corporations in the U.K., spending in excess of £50,000 each per annum on vehicle rental.

3. Reservations

The Reservation Department based at the Hatfield head office acts as a central point through which private and Corp Rate reservations are passed out to licensees. International Reservations for the U.K. are received via a telex link with the worldwide Budget Reservations computer centre in Omaha, Nebraska, U.S.A.

4. Image

One of the most important factors of the success of the system has been the correct application of the brand name Budget Rent-a-Car. Location signing and vehicle livery is available for all licensees as are smart uniforms for both male and female staff, which in addition to all the other advertising and promotional material make the name of Budget instantly recognisable not only in the U.K. but throughout the world.

A new licensee receives a specially designed counter unit on free loan, an initial supply of uniforms for his staff, and financial assistance towards the cost of the facia sign for the premises.

5. OPERATING SYSTEMS

A complete business system for vehicle rental is made available as part of the overall Budget package. It comprises everything from rental agreements, fleet controls, and daily operating control forms, through weekly and monthly management controls to profit and loss statements.

Regular digests of operation and financial statistics are circulated to licensees to enable them to check their progress.

6. TRAINING

Complete training courses covering all aspects of vehicle rental including customer qualification (those you should rent to and those you should not) are available free of charge to all rental staff and the courses are RTITB approved. These one-week courses are held at head office where a full and modern training facility is located. Refresher training and other motivational courses held in groups locally as well as personal training on location when required.

7. FIELD MANAGEMENT

A strong field management advisory force consisting of district and regional managers regularly visit and communicate with the licensee and his staff. The team's objective is to assist and advise the licensee on utilising both assets and personnel so that he can obtain maximum profit from his Budget franchise.

8. INSURANCE

The Budget Rent-a-Car System enjoys an insurance programme unequalled within the vehicle rental industry. Placed with General Accident it is a comprehensive policy with contingency and conversion cover and is arranged such that premiums are paid monthly in arrears on a percentage of revenue basis.

9. RATES

Full research into the setting of rates, including continuous monitoring of costs and competitive activity, is carried out at head office, and recommendations are regularly made to licensees.

10. VEHICLE AVAILABILITY

Through a tie-up with British Leyland, licensees enjoy full fleet priority facilities.

11. MARKET RESEARCH

Surveys of the vehicle rental market are carried out both on a regular and an *ad hoc* basis to obtain full information with regard to the changes taking place in the market, so that licensees can be kept informed of any necessary changes in marketing strategy.

Undoubtedly the potential for achieving a good profit exists. The Budget Rent-a-Car System has stood the test of time with existing licensees who have operated Budget Rent-a-Car profitably for several years.

A new licensee is immediately "plugged in" to the System and can enjoy the business that the name Budget Rent-a-Car generates together with the goodwill inherent in the Budget name throughout the world.

The Budget franchise offers the qualified person or business the opportunity to invest in the growing vehicle rental industry whilst retaining the benefits of running his own business.

This combination of the local Budget licensee supported by the expertise of Budget Rent-a-Car (U.K.) Ltd. allows the Budget Rent-a-Car System to offer its customers:

* Newer cars (generally under six months old)
* Comprehensive insurance
* Proper customer service including free local area collection and delivery
* Rates which can save him between 10 per cent and 35 per cent when compared to other international car hire networks

whilst allowing the Budget licensee to enjoy profits which can give him after interest returns of 20 per cent or more on his investment.

Upon examination of this presentation it is seen that the Budget Rent-a-Car franchisee acquires a brand name which is known not merely nationally but also internationally; a name which is supported by national and international advertising. He is given the benefit of experience that would be very costly to acquire. For example, one vital factor in car hire must be to assess the reliability and acceptability of the prospective customer. A Budget Rent-a-Car franchisee is given the benefit of the company's international experience in this area right from the outset. This is something which it would be impossible for him to acquire even at great expense and experience, for even if he were to open on his own he would never acquire such a wide experience as the franchisor has acquired.

Budget Rent-a-Car is able to ensure that the franchisee obtains his vehicles at cheaper prices, is able to advise on the optimum vehicle utilisation and on the disposal of vehicles. Guidance is also given in regard to servicing.

The opportunity exists for the franchisees to co-operate with each other in inter-office bookings and, indeed, inter-continental bookings without using third parties to whom large commissions have to be paid.

The vital pre-opening training and continuing supervision is provided. Additional benefits are obtained by the franchisees by virtue of the bulk negotiating power that is vested in a franchisor of Budget Rent-a-Car's size and scope. From the presentation it is seen that these side benefits include the insurance arrangements (a very important feature of car hire) and repurchase arrangements with car dealers.

Furthermore, there is the advantage for this franchisee in the securing of national, and indeed international business accounts. Budget Rent-a-Car is able to make arrangements with large companies of national or international repute that their car hire requirements will be obtained from the franchisees in the chain. This is the sort of contract that no individual franchisee would be in a position to obtain let alone service. The customer obtains a better service than would be obtained from individual branches of a non-franchised chain as each individual franchisee is so keenly interested in retaining the benefit of the account for the contribution that it would make to his profitability. In addition the franchisee becomes part of the Budget World Wide Reservation System which automatically opens up for him a market to which he would not otherwise have access.

Dyno-Rod—A Potted History and Profile

Drain clearing in the U.K. was traditionally the domain of the plumber. Techniques and methods had not changed since the days of Dickens. But working conditions had, and drain clearing was the "unattractive" end of the plumbing business; it received little priority and the customer just had to wait.

Dyno-Rod changed all that. With the introduction of electromechanical machinery capable of snaking its way through the most torturous of pipework, the likes of which had never before been seen in the U.K., Dyno-Rod set out in 1963 to provide the public with a 24-hour emergency service, 365 days of the year. Dyno-Rod vans were white with bold, colourful insignia, very different from the local plumber. Each vehicle was equipped with machinery capable of dealing with blockages in pipes 1 to 12 inches in diameter and in runs of up to 200 feet long. Dyno-Rod made itself known through the major newspapers; in London's Underground trains and on television—methods unprecedented in the world of the plumber. The response was tremendous and Dyno-Rod's London Service Centre was inundated with calls. For the next two years Dyno-Rod operated the business direct and established a sound base from which to expand.

Marketing philosophy dictated that the Company should expand rapidly—nationally. Circumstances indicated that this objective could be best achieved by franchising.

London was the first "target" for the franchising programme and, because of the advertising which had been taking place, the response to the announcement for "franchisees" soon secured distribution for the Greater London area. Then the national franchise expansion programme began, thus achieving the main objectives:

Overcoming the problem of extensive funding.
Opening the way for rapid but controlled expansion.
Securing dedicated management up and down the country to meet the needs of the public 24 hours a day, 365 days of the year, good weather or bad.

What had these "franchisees" bought?
First, they had bought the right to use the name and operate "the Service" in a protected

territory. They bought into the Dyno-Rod business after much of the risk had been taken out. The system was tried, tested, and proven. They bought into a continuing relationship with the licensor. The relationship was, and is, simple and straightforward.

The franchisor (DYNO-ROD LTD.) grants the licence, provides the know-how and training, and promotes the business continually throughout the duration of the licence.

The franchisee (the party taking the licence) provides the manpower and equipment and operates "the Service" in accordance with the contract. In return for the continuing promotion and management support, the franchisee pays a continuing royalty.

This, in simplistic terms, is the basic relationship. Behind it is a well-honed, smooth-running business machine through which Dyno-Rod Ltd. supports its licensees and develops the business by means of:

1. Extensive advertising on television and radio networks throughout the country.
2. National, regional, and local press advertising.
3. Industrial press advertising.
4. Local promotions, e.g. mailing campaigns, door-to-door distributions, etc.
5. Exhibitions on a national and local scale.
6. Sales promotion materials, e.g. brochures, etc.
7. Field sales support personnel.
8. Public relations activities.
9. External seminars, e.g. for municipal officers, public works engineers, etc.
10. Salesmen's training schemes.
11. Technical advice, information, publications, etc.
12 Financial advice, profitability studies, forecasts, advice on budgeting, etc.
13. In-house communications through house magazines, newsletters, bulletins, etc.
14. Meetings and conferences: visits by HO personnel, committees, and policy groups, spanning administration, pricing and technical matters, regional conferences, annual national conference, and social events.

Dyno-Rod provides one of the most comprehensive support programmes in franchising and Dyno-Rod personnel are frequently called to lecture on this topic to other businesses, large and small.

Together, Dyno-Rod and its licensees have developed a business which has grown on average by 37 per cent each year over the past eight years, advancing from a gross turnover of £325,000 in 1969 to £3,900,000 in 1977 as shown in Table A.

In any partnership, both parties must benefit and the benefits must be equitable.

The relationship between Dyno-Rod and its licensees has proved to be equitable (Table B on page 102).

It will be seen that the franchisee earns a profit of approximately 21 per cent of turnover, whilst return on capital employed is in the order of 100 per cent.

(It was estimated that at the end of 1977, the capital employed at service centre level, i.e. the capital employed collectively by all fifty-two Dyno-Rod licensees, was in the order of £850,000.)

Dyno-Rod management is continually evaluating company performance; anticipating market changes, customer attitudes, technical development and formulating strategies for the future.

Alongside the franchise organisation, Dyno-Rod Ltd. also operates a number of company-owned territories for the purpose of keeping in close touch with the detailed

Table A

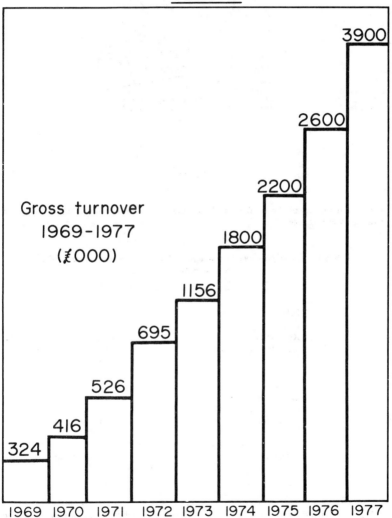

The Revenue 'Cake'

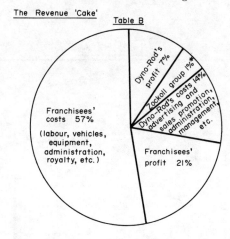

Table B

operational aspects of the business and for testing new ideas, equipment, management techniques, etc. (Table C).

TABLE C. *Typical pro-forma cash flow for a Dyno-Rod franchisee in the £100,000 p.a. turnover Range*

	%
Fees	24.00
Payroll	27.70
Rent and rates	1.20
Vehicle running costs	11.33
Equipment	1.86
General administration	0.97
Utilities	2.00
Legal and professional	0.57
Other costs	2.00
Depreciation	2.23
Finance	5.06
Profit	21.00

* Dyno-Rod Ltd. is a member of the Zockoll Group which is the proprietor of the trade mark "DYNO-ROD". The Zockoll Group also set up "Pit-Stop", the while-you-wait silencer chain and is also engaged on a new concept of car re-spray centres.

Dyno-Rod Ltd., the parent company so-to-speak, is not, therefore, a capital intensive business. It relies on having developed a system and a very strong brand name with extraordinary high brand awareness.

A recent survey carried out by Dr. M. J. K. Stanworth of the Polytechnic of Central London School of Management Studies showed that the public awareness of Dyno-Rod was 79 per cent. Awareness of this high order is normally only achieved in the area of consumer products.

SUMMARY
Some key facts

— 14 years of consistent growth.
— Pioneer and market leader in field of drain and pipe clearing.
— Brand awareness as high or higher than many well-known household products.
— More than just a drain clearing company—process pipe clearing an important aspect of the business.
— More than just a domestic drain clearing service—industrial sector accounts for 70 per cent of business.
— Experts at high pressure/velocity water jetting work.
— Self-contained management team.
— Dyno-Rod provides an essential service.
— Market for the service increases as cost of replacement systems increase.

AREAS FOR GROWTH
1. Continuing growth in the domestic emergency sector.
2. Continuing growth in the industrial/commercial sector.
3. Further growth of the preventative maintenance contract portfolio.
4. Development of the Hygiene Service Division.
5. Development of the Specialist Services, e.g. television inspection, etc.
6. Growth through expansion into new markets, e.g. drain laying, repairing, etc.
7. Licensing of overseas territories.
8. Acquisitions.

This presentation is another good example of the way in which franchising has enabled a company comprising a relatively small team of specialists to expand rapidly. Dyno-Rod very thoroughly tested its scheme before proceeding widely to launch it.

It will be seen that Dyno-Rod receives its income by means of the percentage on gross income calculation. The fee is quite considerable but so are the services provided for the franchisee in return.

An interesting feature is the employment by Dyno-Rod of a team of "industrial negotiators" who are always seeking to arrange for the group to secure the work of large industrial companies. In addition there is the holding of the external seminars which is the sort of service one individual would not find at all viable but which can spread benefits over all franchisees.

In view of the fact that the service provided is one that is not frequently required by individuals, the name must be actively promoted. When someone's drains go wrong they should think of Dyno-Rod and contact them. To this end the Company spends as much as one-half of its income from franchisees on advertising and promotion and on a scale that makes far more impact than could be made by an individual. Indeed, as is pointed out, Dr. Stanworth's field study has demonstrated just how effective this promotional effort has been. It is also interesting to note that the Company as a matter of policy owns and operates its own territories so as to ensure an ongoing practical experience and providing scope for experimentation and innovation.

Table D effectively shows the head office organisation which has developed to service the needs of the Company and its franchisees. Each of the seven branches are directly concerned with service to the franchisee either directly or indirectly and it can be seen how wide is the range of skills to which the franchisee has access for advice. It is also apparent that Dyno-Rod is geared to think about the ways of developing its business in a manner which would not be available to the franchisee if he were on his own.

In studying the tables in Appendix B the following interesting factors can be noted:

PART ONE

Table 2. In a franchise which may be considered a "manual job" only 3 out of the 31 franchisees were previously manual workers.

Table 3. 27 out of the 31 franchisees recognised the value of the franchisors "umbrella" the lowering of risks inherent in establishing a new business or that this was a sound business venture.

Table 6. 27 out of 31 franchisees felt they were given full financial information before signing their contracts.

Table 14. Only 1 franchisee thought that the public understood the relationship with the franchisor although (Table 15) 6 thought that the public saw them as independent contractors.

Table 16. It is somewhat puzzling to find that 5 franchisees thought they were not provided with training while 19 thought that the training was reasonable to excellent.

TABLE D. *Organisational structure, Zockoll Group Supervisory*

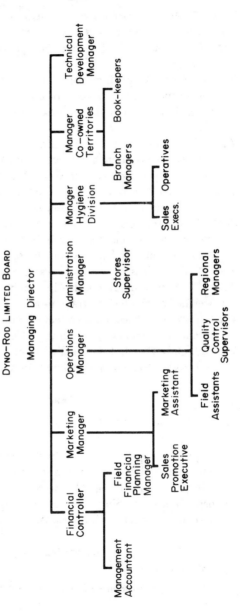

Table 17. On the other hand, 29 out of 31 thought the quality of the equipment supplied was reasonable to excellent.

Table 19. 23 out of 31 consider the operating manual reasonable to excellent.

Table 20. Rather surprisingly for a company about whose services there is an exceptionally high level of public awareness, 10 out of the 31 franchisees thought the national advertising either non-existent or poor.

Tables 22–24. In the areas of technical support and availability and quality of continuing advisory services, two-thirds of the franchisees thought Dyno-Rod's efforts reasonable to excellent.

Tables 27 and 28. The franchisees are quite positive in recognising the value of the brand name to their business.

Table 29. An impressive 25 out of 31 (80.7 per cent) felt that their businesses were more successful because they were franchised (see also question 21 in Part Two of the Appendix).

Table 32. Two-thirds of the franchisees were satisfied with their franchise.

Table 33. Almost unanimously the franchisees consider the contract weighed in favour of the franchisor.

Table 37. 22 out of the 29 franchisees who replied state that their present intention is to renew the contract while only 4 do not intend to do so.

Table 43. Only 4 were dissatisfied with the profitability of their business although one cannot judge the position without more facts.

Part Two

Question 8. 15 out of the 16 Dyno-Rod franchisees who were interviewed "would advise anyone else to do what they have done". This is impressive support for the franchise system, although (question 12) the number drops to 13 when the question is would the franchisees still go into franchising if they were starting today.

Questions 14 and 15. Show a generally high level of satisfaction by franchisees with the relationship between franchisor and franchisee.

Holiday Inn (U.K.) Inc.

The Holiday Inn Story

In 1951 a Memphis home builder, Kemmons Wilson, took his wife, five children, and his mother on a vacation. The inconvenience and high price of family accommodations they experienced made him realise that the lodging business was, as he said, "the greatest untouched industry in the world".

In 1952 Wilson built the first Holiday Inn in Memphis, Tennessee. It was so successful that, within the next year, he built three more inns in the city. And the Holiday Inn story began.

Wilson discussed his Holiday Inn idea with another Memphis home builder, Wallace E. Johnson. Together they visualised a nationwide network of Holiday Inns offering the travelling public suitable accommodations at reasonable rates.

In 1953 they formed a partnership that became Holiday Inns Inc. and was later listed on the New York Stock Exchange. In addition to continuing their building programme, they encouraged other independent business and professional men to develop Holiday Inns through a programme of franchise licensing. Over 75 per cent of the Holiday Inn System of more than 1700 properties in 43 countries has been developed through franchising.

What is a Holiday Inn?

It is a modern hotel facility that offers standardised, quality accommodations and services throughout the world. It embodies a unique concept of hotel marketing and management, especially in that all Holiday Inns are part of an organisation—The International Association of Holiday Inns—known as "The System".

What is the System and how does it work?

The System is the co-operate organisation through which more than 1000 independent businessmen pool their time, talents, and funds in a common endeavour to enable each Holiday Inn to receive marketing power, creative trust, and management guidance that no individual hotel or group of hotels could achieve on its own. Throughout the year, committees made up of franchisees and representatives of Holiday Inns Inc. meet frequently to resolve pressing issues and participate in the formulation of overall strategies. The efforts of these committees along with the fees contributed by each Holiday Inn in the System have brought about such benefits as the largest marketing and advertising fund in the industry (over £10 million in 1975), the first computerised, instant hotel reservation system—Holidex, and the £2.5 million Holiday Inn University.

What is a Holiday Inn franchise license?

It is the binding agreement between Holiday Inns Inc. and the franchisee that, while maintaining proprietorship of his own business, bestows upon the franchisee all the benefits of being part of the Holiday Inn System. The license is granted for a specific site and not for general areas, cities, or countries.

A Holiday Inn franchise represents:
— A brand name with instant recognition, customer acceptance, and goodwill.
— The proven planning, construction, and operating guidelines that have led to the development and operation of more than 1700 Holiday Inns in 43 countries and territories.
— System sales representation throughout the world.
— Referrals to and from more than 1700 Holiday Inns and sales offices through Holidex—the instant worldwide reservation network.
— System advertising exposure on a worldwide basis.

— Exposure to, and a voice in, the affairs of the System through the International Association of Holiday Inns.
— Management counselling and extensive training programmes through the Holiday Inn University.

What is the size of the investment?

The cost of the project which would in 1978 range from £1 million to £10 million depends on the size of the proposed Holiday Inn, the amount of land and its value, the type of building design, the cost of financing, and local conditions. In general, the franchisee's investment should be about 25–40 per cent of total project cost depending on local conditions. Land costs normally represent 10–20 per cent of the total project cost. The site may be owned or leased. Lending institutions normally require leased land to be subordinated to the first mortgage.

Can an existing hotel become a Holiday Inn?

Existing hotels, which meet Holiday Inn standards, are eligible for consideration.

How much land is necessary?

Some of the multi-storey, centre city locations are built on as little as 20,000 square feet. Holiday Inns in outlying areas may require 3–5 acres, and resort properties often require even larger areas.

What assistance can be expected in the development phase?

Site selection: Holiday Inn development specialists will help evaluate sites in the area of interest.

Architecture and construction: a representative of the Holiday Inn Projects Development staff will work with the franchisee and his architect to ensure the most feasible and economic approach to design and structure while preserving local architecture and traditions. The choice of architect and building contractor is the franchisee's subject to approval by Holiday Inns, Inc.

Furnishings and Equipment: all furnishings, fixtures, equipment, and supplies must meet Holiday Inn standards. Items that meet these standards are available from several sources. Holiday Inn's own supply companies can furnish individual items or a furnishings and equipment package.

Project co-ordination: a project co-ordinator will be assigned to the project during the development phase. His attention will ensure that the project meets Holiday Inn requirements.

Development phase inspections: the project will be inspected at least twice during construction, the last inspection serving to verify adherence to standards and to authorise the property to open as a Holiday Inn.

Pre-opening training: Holiday Inn University will train the innkeeper and other key personnel. There is no tuition fee for these courses at the university, but the franchisee will be responsible for transportation, room, board, and other personal expenses. In addition, the university is available on a fee basis to train the entire Holiday Inn staff prior to opening, upon request.

What support can be expected when the Holiday Inn is open and operating?

Advertising: the benefits of a worldwide advertising programme, utilising local, national, and international media, aimed at selling the travelling public the name and image of

Holiday Inns. ∴ his is in addition to the franchisee's local advertising effort, and gives brand name coverage to all Holiday Inns.

Marketing: marketing specialists carry on continuous research, and design numerous programmes and promotions utilized on a systemwide basis. They are available to consult with franchisees concerning specific marketing needs.

Holidex reservation system: Holidex, capable of using undersea cables and communication satellites, enables Holiday Inn customers to make free, instantaneous reservations. The Holidex network is also interfaced with some airline reservation computers, enabling travellers to obtain airline and hotel reservations simultaneously. Holidex terminals are being installed in many large corporate offices for direct reservation service.

Sales and reservation offices: a worldwide network of sales and reservation offices gives all Holiday Inns in the System direct sales representation in many of the world's major cities, thus adding to each Holiday Inn's individual sales effort. Major sources of business, especially travel agents, tour wholesalers, and operators, are aggressively solicited by sales representatives from each office.

Public relations: the Public Relations Department works constantly to place stories and articles about Holiday Inns in the media, and to provide the System and individual Holiday Inns with meaningful promotional programmes.

Training aids: in addition to the innkeeper training during the development phase, the Holiday Inn University supplies the franchisee with constantly updated training films in several languages. The university can also retrain personnel on a fee basis at the franchisee's Holiday Inn. Annual conferences are held each year for the innkeeper and food and beverage director at the university and in some overseas locations.

IAHI world conference and committees: ten committees (marketing/advertising, reservations, rules of operation, construction, education and research, finance, conference, world affairs, legal—legislative, and food and beverage) meet periodically throughout the year to consider and act upon problems and opportunities facing the System. The members of each committee serve voluntarily and are chosen from the IAHI membership by the individual committee chairmen on the basis of individual expertise and the desire of the franchise owners. The world conference is held by the International Association each year for the exchange of ideas and the presentation and implementation of new System programmes.

What fees are currently required of a franchisee.

— A minimum initial franchise fee of £7500 plus £50 for each room over 100 rooms.
— Franchise royalty of 7.5p per room per night, or 3 per cent of gross rooms revenue, whichever is greater.
— Holiday Inn "Great Sign" lease fee of £40 per month. (Additional signs of varying design are optional.)
— Holidex reservation terminal lease fee of £1.50 per room per month.
— System advertising fee of 1 per cent of gross rooms revenue, or 4p per room per night, whichever is greater.
— System Reservations and Sales Office fee of 0.8 per cent of gross rooms revenue or 3p per room per night, whichever is greater.
— Holiday Inn University fee of ½p per room per night.

For the majority of Holiday Inns, the above fees normally amount to less than 6 per cent of gross rooms revenue. No fees are charged on revenues derived from food, beverage or other sources.

What is the process in obtaining a Holiday Inn franchise?

If a prospective franchisee has sufficient funds and a site which he thinks is feasible and wants to pursue a Holiday Inn franchise commitment, he should contact the nearest Holiday Inn franchise office. The franchise representative will want to discuss the following items with him:

— The location of his property.
— The surrounding area—its industries, airport, highway systems, population, labour force, educational facilities, and general economic strength.
— The number of hotels and rooms already operating in the area and their quality.
— The type of group wishing to make application: individual, partnership, limited partnership, corporation.
— Laws regarding franchise licenses which might apply to his area.

After discussing this information in detail, the franchise representative will request materials to assist further in evaluating the proposed site. These materials might include city or highway maps, a plot plan of the specific site, the name of the owner or lessee of the property, cost of the property, names and occupations of individual partners involved in the group, certified financial statements and personal and business references from each member of the group, and any other materials which could be pertinent.

If after analysing this information it appears that the prospective franchisee has a potential Holiday Inn location, the franchise representative will encourage him to prepare a formal application. The formal application consists of the submission of all necessary forms and the payment of the application fee. Once these have been received an on-site study of the project will be made by a representative of the franchise department. At that time he will make recommendations regarding the feasibility study which must be completed prior to the presentation of the application to the Franchise Committee. Independent feasibility studies are required for all new applications. In either case, it is not recommended that a study be commissioned until a representative of Holiday Inns Inc. has had an opportunity to review the location personally.

If the application is approved by Holiday Inns Inc. the prospective franchisee will receive a commitment agreement to issue a license agreement. This document is an interim agreement and provides for the timely development of the project. Once all terms of the commitment agreement to issue a license agreement have been met, construction of the project is complete, and the property receives authorisation to open as a Holiday Inn, a Holiday Inn license agreement is issued. Both the commitment agreement to issue a license agreement and the license agreement itself carry the date of the original approval of the application.

Is the franchisee obliged personally to operate his Holiday Inn?

No. Many franchisees choose to hire management firms for the operation of their Holiday Inns or to lease it to operators. Holiday Inns Inc. must approve all management agreements and leases. Holiday Inns Inc. offers management services through management contracts. Holiday Inn's experienced professionals can provide technical assistance through the development phase of the property and manage it for a franchisee after opening.

The Holiday Inn franchise presentation reveals a franchise which is based on orthodox business format franchise lines. All the elements are present comprising a wide range of services prior to the opening of the business and an extensive continuing relationship thereafter.

Holiday Inns operate in a capital intensive business, and one is left to doubt or to speculate upon the prospects of an individual achieving the exposure of 1700 outlets in 43 different countries within a period of 25 years were it not for the franchise system.

Within that period over 1000 individuals have become involved in establishing hotel businesses throughout the world to a common format and with many common benefits. It is interesting to note that there has been established a co-operative system between franchisees so that their information is pooled and individual experiences can become part of the common fund of information available from each.

The franchisee on taking up a Holiday Inn franchise is immediately put on the map as part of the Holidex instant hotel reservation system which is operated on a worldwide basis and the Holiday Inn literature which is disseminated widely throughout the world makes known its existence and its location. This is something which an individual would otherwise be incapable of achieving. The presentation which is extremely detailed is an effective and impressive demonstration of the application in practice of the principles as explained in this work relating to the establishment and operation of a business format franchise.

Kentucky Fried Chicken

How It All Began
    Kentucky Fried Chicken is the original creation of the world renowned Colonel Sanders. He started out selling meals to travellers from his petrol station in Kentucky, U.S.A., and became so well known that the demand for his cooking swiftly persuaded him to set up a restaurant.
    This operation was highly successful and there he developed his now famous and unique Kentucky Fried Chicken using a secret recipe of 11 herbs and spices. Today the recipe remains unchanged and Colonel Sanders, now in his eighties, is still active in the promotion of Kentucky Fried Chicken, travelling many thousands of miles each year.
    The worldwide success of the Kentucky Fried Chicken business is now well established, with over 5000 stores in over 40 countries. 4000 of these are in the United States of America, the rest being widely spread over the world, with the U.K. being the most important market outside the United States.
Kentucky Fried Chicken in the U.K.
    Kentucky Fried Chicken (G.B.) Limited was formed in 1965. The U.K. network has grown rapidly to more than 250 stores of which 45 are company owned and operated. A Kentucky Fried Chicken franchisee is part of a highly successful fast food retailing operation selling a unique high quality product.

KENTUCKY FRIED CHICKEN—A UNIQUE RECIPE

"Finger Lickin' Good." A well-known phrase that sums up the special nature of Kentucky Fried Chicken. The chicken is cooked by a special method using Colonel Sanders' unique recipe of 11 herbs and spices making it succulent and full of flavour. Kentucky Fried Chicken is offered in stores with a comprehensive range of additional products, including chips and jacket potatoes, fresh coleslaw, barbecue beans, soup, and, of course, chicken sauce. There is also a choice of desserts and soft drinks.

New products are being added to the menu. Barbecue spare ribs, for example, were introduced in 1976. With their distinct tangy flavour, they are making a significant contribution to sales. Regular additions are made to the range of side dishes, sometimes for specific promotional activities, other items for permanent inclusion in the menu.

Presentation is an area in which great pride is taken. The packaging is well designed, visually attractive, and extremely practical in use. All this not only adds up to the best takeaway product in the country but means that one can provide bulk catering for outside functions. This service is rapidly growing as customers find it easy to use, highly acceptable, and very economical. Unique product, unique packaging, unique service all promote corporate awareness and help make our product even more popular. But to sell a good product it is necessary to have good stores.

KENTUCKY FRIED CHICKEN—STORE DESIGN

Stores are designed to be bright, warm, and cheerful. Store design and decoration are the subjects of an on-going development programme, incorporating improvements and additions within the framework of the Kentucky Fried Chicken image.

Every one of the company stores has been completely modernised in the last 12 months and converted to the new "open plan" design with visual cooking. All franchise units are now in the process of being upgraded and improved. No other food organisation can approach Kentucky Fried Chicken's dynamic rate of progress.

Kentucky Fried Chicken restaurants are opening offering seating and dine-in facilities in addition to the regular takeaway service. More restaurants are planned for the future.

Kentucky Fried Chicken is proud to be setting the highest standards in the fast food industry with its stores and service.

ADVERTISING AND MARKETING

Kentucky Fried Chicken is the largest national advertiser in the fast food market. Every franchisee gets all the benefits. He gains from a powerful programme of national TV and radio campaigns, backed up by colourful attention-getting point of sale materials.

There is an advertising board with elected franchisee representatives responsible for the advertising strategy and expenditure.

The Marketing Department provides expert support for the franchisee in the field of advertising, promotional activity (at national and local levels), public relations, and operates a continuous programme of market/customer research and new product testing. It also offers help and advice on sales, image-building, customer relations, merchandising, local "events", and over-the-counter selling.

The Marketing Department is backed up by a top flight front rank national Advertising Agency and no less than two public relations companies who are at the disposal of the franchisee for any assistance he may require. A steady stream of accurate news and feature articles in the top papers, radio, and TV of this country has been a very positive result of this—*The Times, Financial Times, Sunday Times, Guardian, Daily Telegraph, Daily Mail, The Sun*, BBC, LBC, lead item in the very first edition of ITV's Business Programme have all had very good things to say about the benefits of the Kentucky Fried Chicken franchise.

PUBLIC RELATIONS AND COMMUNICATIONS

Kentucky Fried Chicken (G.B.) Limited have a very active public relations strategy retaining two national PR agencies, political advisers, two firms of specialist solicitors, town planning consultants, and surveyors. All of these organisations are available to offer expert advice over the whole range of business problems that may be encountered by a Kentucky Fried Chicken franchisee.

Kentucky Fried Chicken (G.B.) Limited were founder members of two trade bodies to help raise standards and the public's perception—the British Franchise Association and the Take Away Food Federation. Kentucky Fried Chicken (G.B.) Limited involves itself in litter projects with the Keep Britain Tidy Group and has successfully petitioned Parliament on behalf of its franchisees.

There are standing committees composed of franchisees and company executives on purchasing and wages which exist to inform all Kentucky Fried Chicken operators and improve their business. These committees and the Advertising Board meet every 2 months. In addition a National Franchise Conference is held three times a year with a convention (held abroad) once a year to which all franchisees are invited. These meetings help the interchange of ideas and improve the business of each member of the Kentucky Fried Chicken family.

TRAINING AND CONSULTANCY SERVICES

Kentucky Fried Chicken (G.B.) Limited hold a series of intensive courses training all personnel in the technical, administrative, and management expertise necessary for the business to run smoothly and profitably. There is a general management course to teach franchisees and their staff the details of the business, and there is a sales course to train and motivate sales staff.

The department also conducts field training courses anywhere in the U.K. and offers advice to franchisees on training methods and systems. Up-to-date training films, slides, charts, and handouts are also made available to franchisees by the department.

The company also provides advice and assistance in the following areas:

Site finding, location, surveying, and assessment of stores.
Provision of architects' drawings for local council planning permission.
Shopfitting, equipment, and suppliers.
Weekly financial monitoring operation.
Quality, hygiene, and standards control.
Food purchasing and preparation advice.

When a franchisee's store is opened, marketing and advertising will play an essential part in its success.

A STEADY RETURN ON THE FRANCHISEES' INVESTMENT

Although all Kentucky Fried Chicken stores are set up within certain strict standards, there is no such thing as an absolute average store. However, the approximate costs as at Spring 1978 for a standard takeaway store are:

The costs:	£
Option fee	1,000
Shopfitting and equipment	18,000
Solicitors' and architect's fees	600
Essential merchandising	400
TOTAL	£20,000

The return:

As a general guide we have taken a store doing £1750 a week. The figures below give a fair guide as to the breakdown of income.

At this level of turnover the store profit would be approximately £262.50 per week and the capital investment would be returned in under 2 years. Because some of the costs are fixed, profitability, hence return on capital, improves dramatically with increased turnovers.

Sales turnover:		100%
Food and packaging	47%	
Wages	15%	
Royalty	4%	
Advertising	3%	
Rent and rates	6%	
Overheads and Utilities	10%	85%
Profit before Tax		15%

With the rapidly improving store design and ever increasing national advertising, the turnover of Kentucky Fried Chicken stores is currently rising faster than at any time in the company's history. The 45 company stores have *averaged* for each of the last 12 months (to mid-1978) a staggering 40% increase in product and cash sales over last year. In addition, Kentucky Fried Chicken are currently experiencing a boom in new store openings. All new units opened in the last 12 months have had sales of £2000 or more in the first trading week. There is no other company in retailing, food, or franchising achieving anything comparable with these figures.

How the Franchisee Benefits

There are many strong and distinct advantages to be gained by becoming a Kentucky Fried Chicken franchisee.

1. He is part of a big, international family, gaining all the security and backing that goes with it.
2. He is offering a top class product—a market leader.
3. He gets the benefit of professional marketing and advertising expertise at all times.
4. Kentucky Fried Chicken is advertised at national and local levels, giving maximum coverage.
5. All the national advertising is backed up by excellent point of sales programmes, plus public relations coverage.
6. Kentucky Fried Chicken offer a wide range of consultancy services, including help with site selection and development, shopfitting advice, a monitoring service, and service to advise the franchisee on preparation, cooking, and storage equipment.
7. The franchisee and his staff can be expertly trained in all aspects of the business.
8. Kentucky Fried Chicken will help the franchisee build sales, with the benefit of well tried and proven methods.
9. If the franchisee puts in the work and the enthusiasm, the profits will show.

Again we have the presentation of an orthodox business format franchise. The worldwide rate of growth is quite startling having taken place in less than the time that has been taken to establish the Holiday Inn chain. On the other hand, the establishment of each of the stores does not involve the same level of capital as the Holiday Inn operation and the availability of suitable franchisees is undoubtedly the much greater.

The operation is simple, the menu range limited and effort is made to ensure that the limited tasks involved are performed well.

Kentucky Fried Chicken (KFC) is a classic example of the effectiveness of updating the decor, design and eye catching appeal of the stores, in that the complete modernisation of each of its many company stores during the past 12 months has resulted in a 40% increase in product and cash sales over the last year. One of the areas in a franchise transaction in which franchisors find great difficulty is in persuading franchisees to update and modernise their stores so as to retain the freshness of the appeal to the customers. KFC has vividly demonstrated the commercial sense of taking these steps by introducing them into its own stores with remarkable financial success. With this lead the franchisee has every incentive to embark upon the modernisation of his store in order to obtain the financial returns achieved in practice by KFC. How much more effective a form of leadership is this rather than having the situation where one has to rely on strict legal rights and the methods of enforcing them that are available. Nothing could be more damaging to what is effectively to be a continuing "partnership" relationship.

Great emphasis is placed upon advertising marketing public relations and communications and the benefits in these areas for franchisees are self-evident. KFC's training method is soundly based, and it is interesting to note again as in so many other cases that franchisees are regularly called together in order to interchange ideas for the mutual benefit of all the members of the franchise chain.

Prontaprint Limited

Prontaprint operates Britain's largest chain of high-speed printing and copying shops offering a range of simple, small-offset litho printing, photocopying, duplicating, and often a plan copying service. Anything too big for the office copier or too small for the commercial printer, where speed is essential, the Prontaprint Service will fill the gap. By keeping within certain limits and including a full design facility, this need for a service offering speed and quality in relatively small quantities is met.

The first shop was opened in Newcastle upon Tyne in February 1971 and was followed by four more company-owned and operated shops in a short space of time. The first franchise was sold in the second year of trading, and there are now (April 1978) over 50 Prontaprint shops in the U.K. stretching from Aberdeen to Plymouth. New units are continuing to open at a steady rate.

Companies large and small and individuals from all sectors of the community find the Prontaprint Service useful—some more than once a week, others even on a daily basis. Cash flow is excellent and potential returns are available for prospective investors.

Being a "business service" with a prestigious image and sociable trading hours, the Prontaprint franchise generally appeals to the "business executive type" of person, male or female, who, for a variety of reasons, are seeking a business of their own, one which will give security and satisfaction not always available when employed even in large international companies. None of the existing licensees were previously printers; they came from a variety of commercial, managerial, and professional backgrounds. Those with a will to succeed and the ability and willingness to absorb the training provided are ideal potential Prontaprinters.

A typical franchise applicant will probably travel the following route when joining the Prontaprint team:

1. An initial inquiry by telephone or letter which will result in Prontaprint sending a standard brochure, together with financial information.

2. The prospective licensee will contact Prontaprint after having read the literature and arrange to visit several shops to speak to existing licensees and glean from them their feelings about Prontaprint, their service and support, and also whether or not they have regretted becoming Prontaprint licensees. Thus, by selecting any Prontaprint shop anywhere in the country, a prospective "Prontaprinter" can assess, by the reactions of each licensee he visits, any areas of doubt in the methods or claims that are made by Prontaprint Ltd.

3. Having "done his homework" the applicant will then arrange to visit Prontaprint at its head office or will visit one of the regional directors and talk in greater detail. At this stage, several hours are usually spent clearing the uncertainties which are in the mind of the applicant, as well as giving both parties a chance to assess each other, for, after all, the relationship can last up to 10 years or more.

4. Once the applicant is approved and he accepts Prontaprint, Prontaprint swings into action.

5. The town of interest will be investigated by the prospective licensee along with a member of the Prontaprint team who will help assess the potential of the area within the guidelines established by Prontaprint based upon its previous experience, and commence a full search for suitable premises.

6. Once a lease has been finalised, architect's plans are drawn up so that quotations can be obtained for shopfitting work, etc., to the standard Prontaprint design and specification.

7. As soon as the licensee is available, he commences a four-week training course which covers all aspects of running a Prontaprint shop from basic product knowledge to artwork, simple offset printing techniques, customer relations, recruiting staff, basic accounts, sales promotion, use of all ancillary equipment, and many other aspects which are relevant to the running of a successful business.

8. Each new licensee is supplied with a training manual which underlines the substance and features of the course in detail and contains instructions on the systems, etc. This manual is retained for future reference.

9. During the training course he receives an artwork package which provides standard artwork for such things as quotation forms, letterheads, business cards, promotional leaflets, press advertisements, and so on.

10. The licensee spends at least two weeks of the course at an existing shop where he learns to deal with customers, operate equipment, and experiences the different types of work that he is likely to encounter. This prepares him for confident exposure in his own shop once it opens.

11. During training, equipment is ordered, often at preferential discount terms and timed to arrive at the shop on completion of shopfitting.

12. At the end of a course the licensee acquires a corporate package of items which includes till rolls, point of sale material, invoice sets, standard accounting kit, promotional artwork, and many other useful items.

13. Once the shop is fitted out and the machinery is run in, a launch promotion is organised by the Sales Promotion Manager of Prontaprint.

14. On a continuing basis, Prontaprint is regularly in touch with all licensees by telephone, visits and correspondence, feeding out new ideas, innovations and techniques, and assisting in the solution of relevant problems.

15. Regular meetings are arranged for local regions as well as up to two national conferences every year.

16. The licensee has full use of the trade marks associated with the Prontaprint Service.

17. Prontaprint regularly monitor the cost of basic raw materials and implement new price structures when the retail margins become eroded by increases in costs. This is organised at Head Office and information is sent to every shop to ensure that every licensee maintains gross margins.

The above is only a part of the wide range of services and activities which are available to every licensee. Without successful licensees there can be no Prontaprint Ltd., consequently there is a mutual interest to increase sales and the relationship is a continuing one. Prontaprint continuously encourages sales growth, and to support this guarantees to spend the entire Marketing Services Fund (a levy of 5 per cent on turnover) on promoting and developing the Prontaprint Service. This activity manifests itself, for example, by way of advertising for every shop, usually in two categories of Yellow Pages and paid for from the fund. In addition, various items are available from time to time including point of sale material, direct mail shots, give-away items, standard press, radio jingles, and television advertising—these items are either provided free of charge from the Marketing Services Fund or subsidised.

One advantage of a Prontaprint franchise as opposed to an independent business is that, as Prontaprint grows and becomes more and more established and a familiar part of the High Street scene, Prontaprint's marketing and sales promotion activities generate an increasing national awareness to every licensee's advantage.

Other long-term advantages of the Prontaprint franchise are:

1. Special group rates on paper, ink, and other consumables.
2. Group discounts on equipment and leasing facilities.
3. Exchange of news and views at regular local and national meetings.
4. Technology advancement—a sharp watch is kept worldwide on relevant developments and information circulated.
5. Re-negotiation of property leases—comparable figures and negotiating skills available.
6. Introduction to sources of finance.
7. When the need arises, a Prontaprint shop usually sells quicker and for a higher price than a "Joe Bloggs Instant Print Shop" (based on past experience).
8. In the event of unforeseen troubles, help is available, i.e. sickness or holiday relief, etc.

9. The strength of the central Marketing Services Fund is behind each licensee (unit) in the event of unforeseen circumstances making an extraordinary promotional effort necessary.

10. Weaknesses in trading are easily identified and corrected when such an extensive cross section of the same business and branch activities is available to be used as a guide and assist in forecasting.

Prontaprint has innovated not merely a new field in U.K. franchising, but a new concept in business, by having noticed a gap in the market, providing services in the field of printing and copying, and by stepping in to fill it. In the short space of 7 years the franchise chain has developed to over 50 shops and in fact new shops are now opening at a very fast rate and the rate of growth is expected to increase rapidly. It is interesting that five pilot schemes were run before any franchises were sold, and it is interesting to note the source from which the company is obtaining its franchisees.

Again this franchise follows the lines of the orthodox business format franchise with which the reader should at this stage be thoroughly familiar. A full range of initial services are supplied including site selection, training which covers all aspects of running the Prontaprint business, and the provision of a training manual. The inclusion in training of at least 2 weeks' work in an existing shop, providing real practical experience is invaluable as is the opening sales promotion which is organised by the company.

Once the business is opened, there are the continuing services, regular meetings of franchisees on a regional basis, as well as two national conferences every year. The common marketing fund into which payments are made is utilised to promote the franchised chain and achieves for all franchisees a degree of exposure which their own contribution would scarcely achieve for them if they were sole traders without the benefit of the umbrella of the franchise arrangement and the value of the contribution from the other franchisees.

Prontaprint are also proud of the fact that the benefits of the franchise arrangement achieve for its franchisees much more beneficial margins of profitability than could be obtained by a sole trader without their know-how.

ServiceMaster Limited

ServiceMaster has developed the world's largest network of independent franchised businesses engaged in professional cleaning services for homes and offices. Today there are more than 1850 ServiceMaster businesses operating worldwide, with over 75 in the U.K.

ServiceMaster licensees offer a wide range of on-location cleaning and restoration services, including carpet cleaning, furniture cleaning, curtain cleaning, wall cleaning, floor cleaning, smoke and odour removal, and other similar services related to providing and maintaining the appearance and useful life of home and office furnishings and surfaces.

ServiceMaster has been involved in franchising in the U.K. since the early 1960s. The parent company, ServiceMaster Industries Incorporated, a U.S. corporation, entered into a licence arrangement in the U.K. in 1962. Franchising operations worked under that arrangement until 1976, when ServiceMaster Industries Incorporated re-acquired U.K. franchising rights.

ServiceMaster offers a unique franchised business opportunity in that the licensee is not required to purchase and maintain shop premises. ServiceMaster businesses can be operated out of the licensee's home, although many will move to a commercial site as the business grows.

For a total initial investment of £4300 the new licensee receives all the professional equipment, chemicals, supplies, promotional materials, training manuals, and individualised instruction needed to launch his business. Financing up to 59 per cent of the initial cost is available to qualified prospects.

The initial license agreement is for 3 years, and is automatically renewed thereafter. All licensees pay a monthly fee of 10 per cent of gross sales, which covers the cost of on-going technical development, training seminars and field counselling, advertising and promotion, etc.

ServiceMaster provides each licensee with a proven marketing plan. Licensees are taught to obtain business from the home market under the ServiceMaster name and as agents for leading retailers and decorators. They serve the office market on a direct basis. In addition, licensees acquire business through their ability to clean and restore all types of buildings following fires, floods, or other similar occurrences. Licensee individual sales efforts are supported by ServiceMaster staff personnel who are continually seeking endorsements from carpet mills, retailers, fibre manufacturers, multi-location businesses, and insurance firms.

First year licensee turnover has ranged from £4000 to £14,000 depending on the degree of salesmanship and effort the individual licensee puts into the building of his business. The average net profit of a licensee operating out of his home, after depreciation but before an allowance for his own salary, is 53 per cent. Once a business is established, turnover can increase to £30,000 or more at only marginally reduced profit margins.

ServiceMaster licensees require no previous experience in on-site cleaning. As a matter of fact, the company has found that the most successful licensees come from backgrounds far afield from cleaning services.

The key to the success of ServiceMaster over the years has been its training programmes. The company provides the most comprehensive initial and on-going training in the industry. In addition to teaching the technical skills required to perform the variety of services, the company also provides systems to teach salesmanship, book-keeping, management, and advertising and promotion.

ServiceMaster Industries Incorporated has been committed to the concept of helping individuals build strong independent businesses since 1948, when the first U.S. franchise was established. The company believes that customers seeking services for their homes and offices have the most confidence in the independent, local business owner who is backed by the experience and technical knowledge of a large national firm. The ServiceMaster franchise opportunity couples those two concepts to provide maximum customer benefit.

ServiceMaster is a company with a unique business philosophy. From an economic standpoint, ServiceMaster is in business to grow profitably. But profit is not an end in itself. It is the means by which it expands opportunity for people. ServiceMaster is committed to the idea that profitable growth should be used to help people develop, to help them reach their full potential in their personal as well as their business lives.

ServiceMaster has translated this unique attitude into four corporate objectives. For ServiceMaster licensees and employees alike, these objectives are a way of life:

> To Honour God in All We Do
> To Help People Develop
> To Pursue Excellence
> To Grow Profitably

ServiceMaster is yet again another example of the orthodox business format franchise which has the advantage in the early stages of being capable of being operated from the franchisee's home so that he is not involved at a critical early stage in the expenses arising out of the establishment of commercial business premises.

The initial investment is not great and there is a valuable back-up provided by the franchisor. ServiceMaster has been in the franchise business for as long as anyone, the first franchise having been established in 1948, which is the very beginning of the modern business format franchise explosion.

It would appear that one of the keys to the operation of the system lies in the technical aspects in which the franchisee is trained having been advised on the correct equipment and chemicals to utilise in the conduct of the business. It is interesting to note that ServiceMaster are trying to instil in their franchisees a feeling of business philosophy that should underline all they do in not only their business life but also their personal life.

In studying the tables in Appendix B the following interesting factors can be noted:

PART ONE

Table 2. By contrast with Dyno-Rod, 6 out of the 31 ServiceMaster franchisees interviewed had previously been manual workers.

Table 3. 26 out of the 31 franchisees recognised the value of the franchisors "umbrella" and the lowering of the risks inherent in establishing a new business and that this was a sound business venture.

Table 6. 23 out of 31 franchisees felt they were given full financial information before signing their contracts. This means that 8 did not take this view. On the other hand (see Part Two, question 11) all 15 interviewed in depth felt that their original decision to go into franchising was the right one.

Table 17. 29 out of 31 franchisees thought that the quality of equipment supplied was reasonable to excellent. All 31 thought the quality of supplies and the quality of the operating manual was reasonable to excellent. In view of the high emphasis on this aspect of the franchise the franchisees are clearly well served in these respects.

Tables 22–27. In the areas of technical support and availability and quality of continuing advisory services, two-thirds of the franchisees thought ServiceMaster's efforts reasonable to excellent.

Tables 27 and 28. The franchisees are quite solid in recognising the value of the brand name to their business.

Table 29. Exactly the same result as for Dyno-Rod in that 25 out of 31 (80.7 per cent) felt their businesses were more successful because they were franchised (see also question 21 in Part Two of the Appendix).

Table 32. Two-thirds of the franchisees were satisfied with their franchise.

Table 33. As in all cases considered the franchisees are almost unanimous in considering the contract weighed in favour of the franchisor.

Table 37. 24 out of the 29 franchisees who replied state that their present intention is to renew the contract while only one does not intend to do so.

Table 43. As many as 7 out of the 31 franchisees were dissatisfied with the profitability of their business which is a remarkable result considering the replies set out in Table 37 and in reply to question 11 in part two of the Appendix.

PART TWO

Question 8. 11 out of the 15 ServiceMaster franchisees who were interviewed "would advise anyone also to do what they have done" and the number only drops to 10 when the question (question 12) is would the franchisees still go into franchising if they were starting today.

Questions 14 and 15. Remarkably, in the light of some of the other replies and data availability as high a percentage as 40 per cent have some reservations about their relationship with the franchisor. This is difficult to reconcile with the information revealed in Tables 17 to 19.

Wimpy International Limited

WHAT IS WIMPY?

The world-famous Wimpy logo stands for both a product and a place. Wimpy, the product, is a pure beef patty, served in a crisp toasted bun. Only pure beef to a special recipe is used, strictly controlled in manufacture and storage so that it is always of the same high standard. Delicious!

Wimpy, the place, often called a Wimpy Bar, is where Wimpy hamburgers are served. The growth of Wimpy hamburger sales has been dramatic since their introduction to the U.K. in 1955, and they continue to enjoy wide popularity. Hamburgers remain the basis of the highly imaginative Wimpy menu and, in conjunction with a small range of other products, offers an attractive range of meals to satisfy differing tastes with large or small appetites—quickly. The menu is completed by a selection of beverages, pastries, and ice-cream desserts.

Wimpy is, above all, the word which has spelled success to those who have invested in, and supported, this brand name.

HOW DOES THE OPERATION WORK?

The key to the Wimpy international franchise is simplicity.

Although the average Wimpy Bar has approximately 1400 sq. ft. of space, there is no restriction to the size of a Wimpy outlet. It can be as small as 100 sq. ft. for an entirely takeaway operation. In all cases, Wimpy International Ltd. offer specialist advice on utilising all available space to the maximum advantage as well as advising on all technical equipment.

All equipment is geared to efficiency, is simple to operate, and easy to keep clean. Staff need have no previous catering experience. All staff can be trained very quickly by experts from Wimpy International Ltd.

Sound site selection is vital. Wimpy International Ltd. apply stringent assessment criteria based on a complete study of potential sites and on experience gained from sites already opened. Units are usually sited in prime locations in the middle of major shopping centres, working, leisure, and cultural areas, where people gather, are away from home, and are in need of a quick meal or snack at a reasonable price.

WHAT SERVICES ARE PROVIDED?

Wimpy International provide:

The right to use the registered Wimpy International trade mark.

Assistance in finding and evaluating potential sites.

Assessment of the profit possibilities for the site suggested.

A complete layout of the suggested site, including decor scheme and equipment needs.

Advice on opening and publicity.

Training of manager and of staff both before and after opening and particular assistance during the critical opening period.

An operations manual for the successful running of the unit.

Standard calculations in percentages so that the franchisee can compare individual unit running costs with those of other Wimpy Bars.

Regular advertising, promotion, and merchandising support.

Instruction on book-keeping and VAT calculation.

Delivery of deep frozen Wimpy products and of freshly baked Wimpy buns.

A wide range of other products approved by Wimpy is also available at competitive prices.

Regular contact from an experienced operations supervisor who will be able to call upon specialist advice from Head Office for any problem a franchisee may have.

THE WIMPY PROPOSITION

1. Company will examine potential locations and advise on their suitability, and will only accept those sites which, in their experience, are likely to be viable. Wimpy International reserve the right to accept or reject a site after an assessment of its trading potential and the overheads involved. It is not their policy to licence new Wimpy outlets if, in their opinion, they would materially affect the business of an existing unit but they do not accept any restriction on their discretion to licence Wimpy outlets in any location.

2. On acceptance of a site, Wimpy International produce plans for the conversion of premises, give technical advice, and, where necessary, will give assistance in obtaining appropriate planning permissions.

3. Wimpy International provide, free on loan, the equipment for griddling and toasting, together with many advertising items.

4. Advice on the administration and general running of the unit is given by an operations supervisor who will also attend at the opening to supervise generally and train staff, until the operation is running smoothly.

5. The cost of shopfitting, equipping, and conversion is borne by the franchisee who is also responsible for staffing and administration.

6. Wimpy outlets must conform to the layout and specification agreed by Wimpy International so that a high standard of appearance is maintained in all units.

7. The name and trade mark Wimpy belong to Wimpy International Ltd. and a Licence Fee of £750 plus VAT is payable for the use of this trade mark at any one site.

8. The licensing of a Wimpy unit is covered by an agreement between Wimpy International and the licensee for an initial period of 5 years, and this is signed as soon as negotiations for the site are completed. The licence fee is payable on signature of the agreement.

9. At the expiry of the initial 5-year period, the agreement is terminable by 6 months' notice to be given by either party. Within the initial 5-year period, the agreement is terminable if the licensee fails to honour the agreement entered into.

10. If a licensee cannot secure a specific site because the lessor requires a multiple covenant, Wimpy International will consider taking the head lease and sub-letting. They are also prepared to discuss the purchase of freeholds or existing leases, where premiums are being asked.

HOW MUCH PROFIT WILL THE FRANCHISEE MAKE?

Although individual site circumstances will ultimately determine that site's profitability, capital invested would normally be returned within 3 years. An approximate guide to the potential profitability of any site can be determined from the gross profit after food costs, which should be 60 per cent. The approximate percentage of overheads against turnover can be as follows:

	%
Rent and rates	12
Wages, including national insurance contributions	25–27
Other overheads (fuel, insurance, etc.)	8
Food costs	40
Net profit (before tax and depreciation)	13–15

The size of a Wimpy outlet, including service area and wash-up, may vary considerably, but the average size, to provide 75 seats, is approximately 1400 sq. ft. The cost of converting and equipping premises will depend upon the nature of the premises involved and will vary between £300–£350 per seat.

Wimpy International Ltd. point out that these estimates are based on their past experience and that they must emphasise that each site must be assessed individually. Their advice on site selection is based on sound experience, but they cannot guarantee any forecast which is made.

WHO IS LIKELY TO BE A WIMPY FRANCHISEE?

The Wimpy system does not require a franchisee to have any previous catering experience, or even any previous business experience.

The franchisee may be an individual who is looking for the opportunity to exercise initiative and enthusiasm in order to establish his own business, or he may be looking for the opportunity to diversify into the growing fast food catering market.

Above all, he will be prepared to accept the advice and guidance of the franchise company in order to ensure that his hard work will translate his capital investment into a sound and profitable proposition.

The Wimpy franchise is probably the oldest established business format franchise in the U.K. having commenced in business in the 1950s. It operates basically on a limited fast-food menu, and the franchise is built round the Wimpy hamburger and the strength of the trade mark "Wimpy". The list of services provided by Wimpy is a clear summary of the orthodox initial and continuing services to be provided in a business format franchise.

The preceding information summarises the existing Wimpy franchise operation. The company is experimenting with alternative food service systems which will be suitable for high rental city centre sites, and will require a substantially larger amount of capital for the initial investment. The company anticipate that the turnovers which these operations are capable of generating, will provide a return on capital at least as great as any conventional Wimpy outlet.

The Wimpy proposition is clear and concise yet comprehensive. It is interesting that the equipment for griddling and toasting and many advertising items are provided free on loan. This, of course, will reduce the capital cost to the franchisee of establishing his business. The assistance offered by Wimpy in connection with the acquisition of leasehold premises is a very valuable contribution which can enable an individual who is proposing to engage in business for the first time to obtain a site in a location that would otherwise be far beyond his reach.

The Wimpy franchise has been successful for many years and many of the franchisees have earned a good income while operating the business as well as making a substantial capital profit on the disposal of the business in due course. There have also been developed over the years a number of chains of franchised Wimpy outlets operated by individuals or companies.

Having been trading by means of the franchise system of distribution since 1955, the company has acquired a considerable amount of know-how and experience in the field which is demonstrated by their presentation.

In studying the tables in Appendix B the following interesting factors can be noted:

PART ONE

Table 2. The Wimpy franchise attracts almost 50 per cent of previously self-employed and a relatively low number of former manual workers.

Table 3. 28 out of the 50 franchisees recognised the value of the franchisors "umbrella", the lowering of risks inherent in establishing a new business or that this was a sound business venture; 15 (i.e. 28.5 per cent) did not bother to reply.

Table 6. 41 out of 52 franchisees felt they were given full financial information before signing the contract; 8 did not take this view; on the other hand (see Part Two, question 11) 50 out of 51 interviewed in depth felt that their original decision to go into franchising was the right one.

Table 16. Again as with Dyno-Rod there is the puzzling reply that 7 franchisees did not think they were provided with training while 30 (out of 42 replies) thought that the training was reasonable to excellent.

Table 17. 35 (out of 43 replies) thought the quality of the equipment supplied was reasonable to excellent.

Table 18. Only 1 of the franchisees who replied thought the quality of supplies was not very good. The others thought it was reasonable to excellent. In a product based franchise this is a good outcome.

Table 19. 36 out of 47 considered the operating manual reasonable to excellent.

Table 32. 37 out of 50 were satisfied with their franchise.

Table 33. 41 out of the 45 franchisees who replied were of the opinion that the contract was weighed in favour of the franchisor.

Table 37. 32 out of 40 who replied stated that their present intention is to renew the contract while only 5 said they did not intend to do so.

Table 43. 15 out of 50 who replied expressed dissatisfaction with the profitability of the business. This as with ServiceMaster is difficult to reconcile with the replies set out in Table 37, and in reply to questions 8 and 11 in Part Two of Appendix B.

PART TWO

Questions 8 and 11. 19 out of 20 franchisees interviewed stated that they would advise anyone to do what they have done and felt that their original decision to go into franchising was the right one.

Questions 14 and 15. Clearly there is room for improvement in franchisor/franchisee relations or perhaps there is a communication problem. On the other hand, the problems cannot be too fundamental (see Table 37 in Part One).

Ziebart Mobile Transport Service Limited

The strong benefit of the genuine Franchise system are demonstrated time and again by Ziebart (G.B.) Ltd. in the operation of its specialist rustproofing network in the U.K.

Now 104 in number and still developing, each franchise holder is a Ziebart specialist and rustproofing authority in a territory, part of a national and international organisation enjoying the strength of common identity yet, able to use his own entrepreneurial skills, based on an ever-increasing platform of market research and national promotions.

Coupled to the foregoing, Ziebart franchise holders also enjoy the essential requirements of franchise success, good products, knowledge, and assistance.

Ziebart (G.B.) Ltd. provide the best sealant technology, can formulate patented tooling, comprehensive technical manuals, and disciplined training, supported by quality control.

In acquiring a Ziebart franchise, the buyer goes through several stages, following his initial inquiry, since the buyer and, equally importantly the company, want the right mix.

1. In response to the inquiry, comprehensive information describing the franchise, the process, the services, the cost, are supplied.
2. Contact is made to determine that the information has been received and to carry out an initial assessment of the person or firm concerning their background, business experience, access to premises, and financial status.
3. If interest remains high, a discussion/presentation is conducted and all the buyer's questions and queries are answered at this point.
4. The buyer is supplied with a Ziebart licence agreement with the advice to have the documents scrutinised by his solicitors on his behalf.
5. The buyer is invited to visit other Ziebart Centres *by himself* and have unhindered discussion with other licence holders.
6. Thereafter, in an on-going situation, the buyer is invited to visit Ziebart Headquarters, meet directors/management, and inspect the back-up service departments within the company.
7. With his interest now translated into a real determination to proceed, the buyer completes the process by signing a previously examined and engrossed document, which clearly describes each party's responsibilities, rights, and privileges. This done, a

launch programme of development activity is prepared and put into action. What does the Ziebart licence holder get in return for acquiring the licence to an agreed area, at the previously published and current figure of £5100 before taxes?

ZIEBART LICENCE LAUNCH PACKAGE INCLUDING EQUIPMENT, MATERIALS, MARKETING, SERVICES

1. Sealant.
   (a) Two barrels XL5TH.
2. Equipment and Literature.
   Schedule A Tooling.
   Schedule D tooling.
   Delivery on above.
3. Technical training (2 persons).
4. Technical manual.
5. Field technical training (3 days).
6. Field sales training (5 days).
7. Station signs (£ for £ contribution with licensee).
8. Launch advertising (£ for £ contribution with licensee).
9. Guarantee insurance (initial premium).
10. Ziebart licence fee.

BENEFITS TO THE ZIEBART LICENCE HOLDER

Exclusive use of the Ziebart name and trade mark as described in the licence agreements; indeed, he is encouraged to use them in becoming the rustproofing authority in his area.

Spontaneous research awareness of the Ziebart name in motoring circles is over 60 per cent; with prompting the figure rises towards 80 per cent.

Exclusive use of patented Ziebart Sealant, tooling, manuals, plus a detailed theoretical and practical training course, enabling him to produce AA approved quality rustproofing.

On-site technical services during his opening period, complemented by continuous quality control programmes and technical up-dating.

Field sales activity at all levels—national commercial contracts, assistance with sales presentations, and access to dealer service representatives in his own territory.

Participation in marketing programmes national, regional, based on an annually increasing promotional budget, embracing national press, televised sports stadia, local radio, and consistent editorial publicity.

Plus the benefit of acquiring sales literature, exhibition materials, geared down to large production runs, producing competitive unit prices.

Access to Ziebart customer profiles both on his own station and nationally, plus national market research studies into the attitudes of motorists towards rustproofing.

In short, wherever the Ziebart licence holder is located, he enjoys the benefits and strength of a national corporate image but is master of his own shop, participating by zone and national dealer meetings in the total operation.

Further, the Ziebart Licence Holder *does not* pay any outgoing royalty, having paid the initial package £5100 to use the Ziebart name and purchasing Ziebart Sealant, this provides the income for the company to operate, generate, maintain its position as market leaders in the U.K.

The Ziebart franchise, which is operating on the field of automobile services, is one of the few such franchises available in the U.K. This is somewhat surprising since with the number of motor-vehicles on the road, one would have anticipated or expected many more motor-vehicle services would have developed to the point of franchising. Ziebart, which is a franchise which has its origins in America, has developed quite rapidly, and the franchise affords to its franchisees very considerable benefits. The value in the name Ziebart in the period of time since its establishment is quite considerable, and the fact that the company's rust proofing has obtained the seal of approval of the Automobile Association must be a considerable advantage for the franchisees. This certainly is a benefit which no individual on his own would have been able to achieve. Ziebart charges for the supply of sealant to the franchisee and does not charge any royalty.

The initial "launch package", which includes the training, also provides·for Ziebart to contribute towards station signs and launch advertising on an equal basis with the licensee and to pay the initial guarantee insurance premium. Ziebart also have a team of dealer service representatives seeking actively to obtain business for the franchisees. This is another business which enables national commercial contracts to be arranged on behalf of the franchisees. There is a continuing marketing exposure which is organised by Ziebart as well as market research studies.

Ziebart's franchisees on opening up for business are established as providing an AA approved service and as being considered experts in the field of vehicle rustproofing. This is the sort of status which an individual not operating under the franchise umbrella would take some years to achieve if, indeed, he were capable of achieving this at all.

CHAPTER 12

How To Enter the U.K. Market from Abroad

IN DECIDING to enter the U.K. market a number of questions will have to be considered, whether or not the proposed business is to be carried on by means of franchising. Basic business decisions have to be taken whether or not franchising is involved. The first fundamental question to resolve is Is the market right?

A survey of the market has to be made taking note of the different social habits, differences in attitude, differences of taste, and so on that exist between the two countries concerned.

One factor that has to be taken into account, particularly by Americans seeking to enter the U.K. market, is that the U.K. must be treated by them as a foreign country. It is so easy for the American to assume that because the same language is spoken (perhaps it would be more accurate to say a similar language) that everything else will be the same. There are considerable differences between English attitudes and values and American attitudes and values.

With this in mind, when consideration is given to the introduction of specialised franchise schemes, a decision will have to be made as to whether or not such specialised services would attract sufficient demand in the U.K. Part of that decision will be to judge whether one can afford to invest in the hope and expectation that the demand can be stimulated sufficiently. Food franchises may offer challenges in this respect and consideration must be given to the differences in eating habits. The risks that are inherent in starting to franchise a business in this country which is well accepted and widely successful overseas but which is not yet established in the U.K. must be very carefully costed and taken into account.

Consideration must be given to whether sufficient volume can be created to enable the concept which has succeeded overseas to be sustained within the U.K. Consideration must be given to what adaptations should be undertaken so that it can successfully operate in the U.K. It may have to operate on the basis of a lower package selling price and a lower volume of sales to ensure economic viability.

New criteria may have to be established for the judging of the sites, certainly road side locations which are such a widespread feature of franchising in the U.S. are not at any time likely to be successful within the U.K. on any sort of scale.

The market will have to be investigated so that an equipment package may be prepared and set up. The cost of obtaining equipment available within the U.K. by comparison with that available elsewhere has to be investigated as do shopfitting costs. All these are factors which have to be taken into account in assessing the viability of the scheme and calculating the package cost to the franchisee. On this basic cost to the franchisee will depend the ultimate return.

Arrangements will also have to be made for the establishment of suitable training facilities within the U.K. so that any necessary training may be given. Of course, the whole of the company's literature will have to be amended so that it takes into account the differences that arise. Training and operational manuals will have to be changed.

In fact these differences as well as the considerations which follow may price a scheme out of existence or render essential a completely fresh approach.

Having decided that the market will admit the proposed business and the scheme it is necessary for the franchisor as is advocated in Chapter 5 to set up his pilot operations and the fact that he has a proven success in the country of origin does not release him from the obligation thoroughly to market test his proposed franchise package on the ground in the U.K. and at more than one location.

He must start again from the beginning and will have to decide from a taxation point of view what is the best way to set up his business interests in the U.K. and will have to consider the effect of corporation tax, perhaps capital gains tax and capital transfer tax not only on himself but on his franchisees, for he will be setting himself up as an expert and he cannot involve franchisees in a scheme which may have inherent taxation problems. He would be wise thoroughly to investigate the alternatives available to him to enable him to minimise his U.K. liability to tax and he will also be well advised to study the double taxation agreements between the U.K. and overseas countries to choose the best route into the U.K. from a tax point of view.

Value added tax will also have to be considered as will its effect on the pricing of the package and in the setting up of the accounting side of the business. If the franchisor originates from a country which does not have a system of valued added tax or similar tax, he will have to come to terms with it in the operation of the system and how it might affect his franchisees.

If the franchisor company is to be controlled by persons who are non-resident in the U.K., consent will be necessary under the Exchange Control Act 1947 for the establishment of their business in this country. Consent is obtained by application to the Bank of England which is normally made by either bankers or solicitors and does not normally present difficulties, although, of course, there may be restrictions imposed on the sources from which the foreign control company may borrow its funds or obtain its capital. The general policy is to welcome investments in England by non-residents provided that these are appropriately financed. Permission for such investments is normally given on condition that subscription or consideration monies are paid either in sterling from an external account or in foreign currency and that any subsequent finance is provided in foreign currency or external sterling at least in proportion to the non-resident interest in the U.K. business. Subject to proper provision having been made for U.K. liabilities including taxes, permission is normally given for the transfer of dividends to non-resident shareholders representing trading profits and investments income. In the event of the sale or liquidation, proceeds may be repatriated provided adequate provision has been made for U.K. liabilities.

The franchisor should also become familiar with the methods and sources of financing that are available in the U.K. There is, of course, a very active international financial and currency market in London, and it is not usually difficult to obtain any necessary assistance, although the availability of funds does fluctuate and the market tends to deal in rather high minimum sums. However, there is also a well-organised and sophisticated market for funds within the U.K. and the obtaining of finance for franchisees should not be a problem provided that there is a demonstrably ethical franchise which has been thoroughly market tested.

The franchisor will also have to turn for advice about the property market to one of the many specialised firms of surveyors. There is a very highly developed property market in the U.K. and it is essential as in so many cases to have the best professional advice available so that an adequate flow of suitable prime locations can be obtained for the site of premises from which franchisees are expected to trade.

The franchisor will also have to familiarise himself with the provisions of the Town and Country Planning Laws which regulate the development and use of land and buildings. This is a highly technical field of law, but the franchisor's U.K. surveyor or lawyer should be able to provide the necessary guidance in this field as also would his architect if he employs one.

Again, while on the subject of property, the franchisor will have to familiarise himself with the security of tenure provisions in the Landlord and Tenant Act 1954, which apply to business premises and the technicalities involved. If the franchisor is to be involved in dealing with real estate he must know the ground rules that apply to such transactions in the U.K.

It is one thing to have the best professional advice available, but it is quite another thing and absolutely essential that the franchisor or any business man for that matter, who is involved with these matters should have a good working knowledge. There will always be times when he will have to know that a potential danger exists for his professional advisers will not be sitting in his office with him every day of the week.

There has been of late a rapidly growing volume of legislation dealing with employment. The franchisor will again have to familiarise himself with these provisions since again he may have to advise the franchisee in relation to the provisions of the various Acts of Parliament dealing with unfair dismissal, redundancy, and employment protection. In addition to this, certain specialised trades, e.g. the catering trade, have their own peculiar problems so far as staff are concerned, and again the franchisor must become thoroughly familiar with the way in which these matters are dealt with in the U.K. It may be necessary for the prospective franchisor to obtain a work permit to enable him to "import" his qualified staff into the U.K. to establish his business.

Many franchisors will come from overseas territories in which there are stringent and effective anti-trust laws. The anti-trust laws in the U.K. are not as stringent as many that exist elsewhere but they do exist. There are the Restrictive Trade Practices Acts which affect both the provision of goods and services and the Resale Prices Act which basically prevents the imposition of a fixed resale price for goods. Then, in addition, there are the provisions of Articles 85 and 86 of the Treaty of Rome which now that the U.K. is a member of the European Economic Community have the potential to affect franchise transactions just as much as they may affect any other business transaction in which anyone in the U.K. may now become involved.

One cannot emphasise too much to any overseas business man intending to trade in the U.K., and this must be a general basic principle involved and inherent in a trading in any territory. It is essential that you become thoroughly familiar with the business laws practices and procedures prevailing. It is of no use to bemoan continually the fact that it is different from that with which one is accustomed. If one seeks to trade within any territory one must play the game according to the rules that prevail in that territory. One must therefore have proper professional advice as well as basic general knowledge. One's professional adviser will undoubtedly and invariably go to lengths to see that one does acquire the basic knowledge that is required.

It will be appreciated that it is difficult in work of this nature and with considerations which of course fluctuate from time to time to give detailed answers to specific problems. This chapter may serve as a useful guideline for any companies or individuals proposing to enter the U.K. for the purpose of establishing franchise or indeed any other business.

The British Franchise Association Limited

THE material contained in this Appendix, save for any comments or explanations which are the author's, has been supplied by the British Franchise Association.

The main objects are defined in the Association's Memorandum of Association in the following way. It will be noted that these objects incorporate the definition of franchising commented on in Chapter 1.

3. The objects for which the Association is established are the following:

(1) To promote, protect and further the interests of franchisors that is, those who in the course of their business grant a contractual licence (a franchise) to another party (the franchisee) which:

(a) permits or requires the franchisee to carry on during the period of the franchise a particular business under or using a specific name belonging to or associated with the franchisor; and

(b) entitles the franchisor to exercise continuing control during the period of the franchise over the manner in which the franchisee carries on the business which is the subject of the franchise; and

(c) obliges the franchisor to provide the franchisee with assistance in carrying on the business which is the subject of the franchise (in relation to the organisation of the franchisee's business, the training of staff, merchandising, management or otherwise); and

(d) requires the franchisee periodically during the period of the franchise to pay to the franchisor sums of money in consideration for the franchise or for goods or services provided by the franchisor to the franchisee; and

(e) which is not a transaction between a holding company and its subsidiary (as defined in section 154 of the Companies Act 1948) or between subsidiaries of the same holding company or between an individual and a company controlled by him.

(2) Without prejudice to the generality of sub-clause (1):

(a) to formulate and to establish or to adopt a code or codes or proper business conduct for franchisors and to promote and to secure their compliance with the same and with high standards of business conduct generally.

(b) to consider and to advise and decide upon and generally to deal with all questions and problems connected with or concerning franchises and the carrying on of business by means of the same; and to promote acceptance of and compliance with such advice and decisions.

(c) to promote trust and confidence in the franchises granted by members of the Association.

(d) to inform and to educate in relation to franchises and on all matters concerning the same.

(e) to promote and secure co-operative action on the part of franchisors in advancing their common interests.

(f) to promote business usages and activities likely to increase the efficiency and economy of the carrying on of business by means of franchises.

The Association in a "hand out" describes its aims, objectives, and activities in the following manner:

THE BRITISH FRANCHISE ASSOCIATION was formed in 1977 by a number of leading British and International companies engaged in the distribution of goods and services through independent outlets under franchisee and licensee agreements. The aims of the BFA include establishing a clear definition of the ethical franchising standards to assist members of the public, press, potential investors and government bodies in differentiating between sound business opportunities and any suspect investment offers.

The BFA will provide a "forum" for the interchange of information and franchising expertise amongst members and the public, through an advisory information service designed to assist potential franchisees in making a judgement prior to selecting a final investment.

Future objectives include establishing approved education programmes, assisting with arbitration procedures and acting as a common voice in liaison with government bodies where legislation exists or is likely to be formulated.

All BFA members have to conform to a stringent code of Business Practice, and have to undergo a detailed accreditation procedure prior to acceptance as a full member.

The BFA acts as a "spokesman" for responsible franchising and represents a number of expanding sections of British business.

Top executives from member companies bring a broad base of expertise and insight to their roles as officers of the BFA providing an able and qualified leadership.

Member companies operate in diverse areas, sometimes as competitors, but all have a proven track record as successful franchisors combined with a genuine faith in franchising as a system capable of serving the public and industry with economy and responsibility.

ACTIVITIES

The BFA holds regular meetings for the interchange of information and expertise between members. Nominated delegates attend International seminars and report on their findings to all members.

A comprehensive programme of events is being planned which will include seminars and conferences covering topics of interest to the membership and various sectors of the public.

Lawyers are retained to act on behalf of the BFA and its members where legislative changes are liable to affect ethical franchising.

An active public relations programme maintains close liaison with the media, trade press, national and provincial newspapers, magazines, radio and television, etc. to ensure they are advised of BFA activities and its views of legislative and administrative proposals.

The BFA also maintains a high level of contact with overseas franchise associations and was provided with valuable assistance during its formation from the U.S. based International Franchise Association.

In accordance with the clause 3(2)(a) of the Association's Memorandum of Association it has adopted a code of ethics to which all members are obliged to subscribe and to observe in or about the conduct of their business. The code is as follows:

CODE OF ETHICS

1) The BFA's Code of Advertising Practice shall be based on that established by the Advertising Standards Association and shall be modified from time to time in accordance with alterations notified by the ASA.

   The BFA will subscribe fully to the ASA Code unless, on some specific issue, it is resolved by a full meeting of the Council of the BFA that the ASA is acting against the best interests of the public and of franchising business in general on that specific issue, in this case the BFA will be required to formally notify the ASA, setting out the grounds for disagreement.

2) No member shall sell, offer for sale, or distribute any product or render any service, or promote the sale or distribution thereof, under any representation or condition (including the use of the name of a "celebrity") which has the tendency, capacity, or effect of misleading or deceiving purchasers or prospective purchasers.

3) No member shall imitate the trademark, trade name, corporate identity, slogan or other mark or identification of another franchisor in any manner or form that would have the tendency or capacity to mislead or deceive.

4) Full and accurate written disclosure of all information material to the franchise relationship shall be given to the prospective franchisees within a reasonable time prior to the execution of any binding document.

5) The franchise agreement shall set forth clearly the respective obligations and responsibilities of the parties and all other terms of the relationship, and be free from ambiguity.

6) The franchise agreement and all matters basic and material to the arrangement and relationship thereby created, shall be in writing and executed copies thereof given to the franchisee.

7) A franchisor shall select and accept only those franchisees who, upon reasonable investigation, possess the basic skills, education, personal qualities, and adequate capital to succeed. There shall be no discrimination based on race, colour, religion, national origin or sex.

8) A franchisor shall exercise reasonable surveillance over the activities of his franchisees to the end that the contractual obligations of both parties are observed and the public interest safeguarded.

9) Fairness shall characterise all dealings between a franchisor and its franchisees. A franchisor shall give notice to its franchisee of any contractual breach and grant reasonable time to remedy default.

10) A franchisor shall make every effort to resolve complaints, grievances and disputes with its franchisees with good faith and good will through fair and reasonable direct communication and negotiation.

The Association has adopted a rigorous policy of investigating applications for membership as it recognises that the Association's reputation can only in the long run be sustained by the ethical standards and behaviour of each individual member. A member whose conduct falls below these standards will not merely damage himself but all other members of the Association.

The Association's current form of application for membership is in the following form:

BRITISH FRANCHISE ASSOCIATION LTD.
Application for Membership
PART I

QUALIFICATION

1. Members shall be actively engaged in the franchise system of distribution of goods and services.
2. Members shall have established and be operating an ethical franchise network which shall be based on sound business principles, and providing a genuine and adequate service to both franchisee and consumer.
3. Members will be required to demonstrate to the Accreditation Committee the intention to provide, on a continuing basis, the service offered to the franchisee and, where relevant, to the public. The viability of the operation, both with respect to the franchisee and the franchisor, must also be demonstrated.
4. Members will be required to satisfy the Accreditation Committee that the systems established by the member company are adequate to protect both the public and the franchisee, where money is advanced in anticipation of a service to be provided at a future date.
5. The member company shall give an absolute undertaking that it will subscribe to the Code of Ethics adopted by the British Franchise Association.

This Code of Ethics draws heavily on the Code established by the International Franchise Association and on the Code of Advertising Practice established by the British Advertising Standards Authority (ASA). Members also have to complete the following Declaration:

DECLARATION & APPLICATION:
   We, the applicant company...Ltd.,
give our undertaking that we are prepared at all times to subscribe to the Code of Ethics adopted by the British Franchise Association. We declare, to the best of our knowledge and belief, that the franchise system we offer is based on sound business principles and provides a viable and ethical business opportunity for the franchisee and a genuine end-product or service for the customer. It is our belief that the systems we operate,

satisfactorily protect both the franchisee and the consumer and, accordingly, we hereby apply for membership of the British Franchise Association:

Signed ....

For and on behalf of .... Ltd.

Registered Office ....

Position held ....

Date ....

The Form shall be signed by the Chairman or Managing Director of the Company making the application.

Application for Membership
PART II—DATA SHEET

SECTION A: COMPANY INFORMATION:

    Name of Company ....

    Name of designated representative...

    Position in Company...

    Address for correspondence...

    Telephone ....

    Chairman of Company..

    Managing Director ....

    Other Directors ....

    Name of Parent or Holding Company.....................................

    Names of Subsidiary Companies..

    Registered name of franchise ....

SECTION B: SERVICE INFORMATION:

    Nature of service provided by the Company thro' franchisees & Company-owned outlets

    ....

    ....

    Date your Company first offered this service............................

    Date of opening the first detached company station..................

    Date of opening the first franchised outlet ....

    Number of franchised outlets operating ....

    Number of company outlets operating ....

SECTION C: REFERENCES:

    Names, Addresses & Telephone numbers of *three* established franchisees:–

    1. ....

    2. ....

    3. ....

    Bank..

    Auditor ....

    Solicitor..

    Trade   1) ....

           2) ....

SECTION D: CONTRACTS:

Please attach copies of current Contracts & Licences: please note any changes under consideration or planned, which you consider to be relevant to future operations. Also kindly enclose with your Application Form any Promotional Literature used in your relationship with

a) Potential Licensees.

b) The Consumer.

Please enclose copy of logo and/or registered trade mark.

In considering the Association's objectives, the first factor of note is that it is established "to promote, protect and further the interest of franchisors". Quite clearly, while it is an Association of and for franchisors, however, it is of interest to examine the specific ways in which this objective is to be achieved.

Firstly, the Association has established a code of ethics "for the proper business conduct for franchisors and to promote and to secure their (franchisors') compliance with the same and with high standards of business generally". The provisions of the code of ethics are undoubtedly calculated to afford protection to franchisees or would be franchisees in their dealings with franchisors.

Paragraphs 2 and 3 afford protection against misleading or deceiving franchisees. Paragraph 4 requires full disclosure of all material information before any binding contract is signed.

Paragraphs 5 and 6 regulate the form and procedure to be adopted in relation to the contents of franchise agreements.

Paragraph 7 requires the franchisor to act responsibly in the selection and approval of franchisees.

Paragraph 8 requires the franchisor to provide the "trouble shooting" services to the franchisee in the interests not only of both parties but also in the public interest.

Paragraphs 9 and 10 touch upon similar aspects of the continuing relationship between the franchisor and franchisee and require fairness, good faith, and goodwill to be shown by the franchisor to the franchisee in all their dealings and, in particular, in the case of alleged breaches of contractual obligations and complaints, grievances, and disputes.

If members do comply with and observe the express provisions and the spirit of the code of ethics it is obvious that franchisees will obtain the benefit of the code. What, then, will happen if a franchisor fails to line up to the standards required by the code? The Articles of Association of the

BFA contain a fairly extensive disciplinary procedure. It is of interest to list the grounds upon which disciplinary action may be initiated which are contained in Article 75.

> 75. Disciplinary action may be taken against any member who:
>   (i) commits a breach of any code of proper business conduct adopted by the Association or with which the Association in General Meeting resolves that the members of the Association should comply; or
>   (ii) is otherwise guilty of illegal business conduct or of business conduct which in the opinion of the Association or of the Council is improper or unfair; or
>   (iii) commits any act of or involving fraud or fraudulent or negligent misrepresentation; or
>   (iv) makes any incorrect statement in or in relation to his application for membership of the Association; or
>   (v) fails to comply with an undertaking required of him by the Council pursuant to Article 84 below; or
>   (vi) is guilty of conduct which in the opinion of the Association or of the Council is likely to bring the practice of franchising or the Association into disrepute.

The undertaking to be given under the provisions of Article 84 is one which may be required by the Council from a member as a result of a disciplinary proceeding. Presumably, this procedure would be used in a case where a franchisor could make recompense in a particular case or would be required to vary a practice or procedure which had been the subject of a valid complaint under the Association's disciplinary procedure.

The Articles establish a detailed procedure providing an opportunity for the member against whom a complaint is made to defend itself. The ultimate decision is made by the Council of the Association in accordance with the requirements of Articles 84, 85, and 86, which are here reproduced.

> 84. The Council in disciplinary meeting, having considered the material and representations put before it, may:–
>   (i) reject the complaint; or
>   (ii) if they determine that the member who is the subject of the complaint has been guilty of an act or conduct within Article 75 above:–
>   (a) require the member concerned to give such written undertaking to the Association as the Council shall think fit;
>   (b) suspend the member concerned for such period (not exceeding eighteen months) as they consider appropriate; or
>   (c) expel the member concerned from the Association.
> 85. If a member shall refuse to give a written undertaking required of him pursuant to Article 84 above, the Council may, after giving the member concerned an opportunity to

make representations to it orally or in writing, suspend him for such period (not exceeding eighteen months) as they consider appropriate or expel him from the Association.

86. Decisions of the Council in Disciplinary Meeting other than a decision to expel a member shall be taken by a simple majority and the Chairman shall in case of an equality of votes have a second or casting vote; a decision to expel a member from the Association shall require a majority of two-thirds of the members of the Council present and voting.

A member against whom an order for expulsion is made, has a right to appeal to all the members in General Meeting.

The code of ethics, coupled with the disciplinary procedure, provide powerful weapons to the BFA which should enable it to ensure the maintenance by members of high ethical standards. How well in practice the BFA will succeed, will depend upon:

(a) its skill in investigating applications for membership so as to ensure that no questionable franchisors are admitted;

(b) the observance by its members of the code of ethics in principle and in spirit;

(c) lastly, but by no means the least, the status that the BFA can achieve in the eyes and minds of the general public. Unless the status of membership of the BFA can demonstrably be important and of value to franchisors, the sanction of disciplinary action or expulsion will be of limited value.

The other specifically stated objectives of the Association are concerned with the promotion of franchising as a concept, the promotion of trust and confidence, the education of the public, the promotion of co-operative action by franchisors; in fact, the usual activities common to all trade associations.

If the BFA can achieve its stated objectives it will make a valuable contribution to franchising in the U.K. and in Europe.

APPENDIX B

Statistical Survey of Selected
Franchises

List of Tables
PART ONE

PART TWO
Section One—The Decision to become self-employed

11.   Did franchisees still feel their original decision to go
              into franchising was the right one?
12.   If franchisees were starting in business again today
              would they still go into franchising?
13.   How long did franchisees think they would continue
              in their present businesses?

Section Two—Relationships with Others

14.   Did franchisees encounter any problems in their
              relationships with their franchisors?
15.   Did franchisees feel that their franchisor gave a fair
              service for the return he got from them?
16.   Did franchisees think the public was generally aware
              that ServiceMaster/Dyno-Rod/Wimpy was fran-
              chised?
              If "yes" did they think it affected their attitude
              towards franchisees' businesses?
17.   Did franchisees think their franchisors made any
              attempt to inform the public that Service-
              Master/Dyno-Rod/Wimpy was franchised?
18.   Did franchisees' customers generally realise that they
              worked for themselves?
              If "no" did they tell them?
19.   How well did franchisees think their brand name was
              known to:
              (a) the general public;
              (b) their potential customers.
20.   Was the brand name ServiceMaster/Dyno
              Rod/Wimpy important to franchisees' businesses?
21.   In franchisees' opinions, were their businesses more
              successful as a result of being franchised than they
              would otherwise have been?
22.   Did franchisees feel that there was less risk in running
              a franchised business than in running a totally
              independent business?
23.   Did franchisees have employees working for them?

24.   Did franchisees find the task of organising other people satisfying?
25.   Did franchisees have problems obtaining staff?
26.   Did their employees know they were franchisees? If "yes" did this affect their attitude to working for them?
27.   Did franchisees experience any problems in their relationship with customers?

Section Three—Advantages and Disadvantages of Franchising

28.   Were there any aspects of franchising that franchisees did not like?
29.   Were there any benefits franchisees' customers got from them as a franchise that they would not have got from an ordinary managed branch of a large company?
30.   Were there any ways in which franchisees could perhaps have given their customers an even better service but could not because of restrictions in their agreements with their franchisor?

APPENDIX B

Statistical Survey of Selected Franchises

Introduction

THE following tables have been drawn selectively from a recent research study into franchising by Dr. John Stanworth of the School of Management Studies, Polytechnic of Central London. The study was based on three leading franchise operations in Britain: Wimpy, Dyno-Rod, and ServiceMaster.

(1) Recorded in-depth interviews with key franchisor executives.
(2) Recorded in-depth interviews with a sample of 51 franchisees.
(3) A mailed questionnaire to a larger sample of franchisees (total number of respondents = 114).
(4) A questionnaire survey of over 200 respondents currently considering entry into self-employment.

The tables which follow are drawn largely from stage 3 (above) of the research but are supplemented with additional tables drawn from data gathered from stage 2.

Part One
Mailed Questionnaire to sample of Franchisees

TABLE 1. *Qualifications gained at the end of secondary education*

	ServiceMaster	Dyno-Rod	Wimpy	Total
	%	%	%	%
CSE	2 (6.5)	— —	1 (1.9)	3 (2.6)
School Certificate/ O-Level GCE	9 (29.0)	12 (38.7)	25 (48.1)	46 (49.4)
Higher School Certificate/A-Level	5 (16.1)	5 (16.1)	10 (19.2)	20 (17.5)

148

TABLE 1. (*cont.*)

	ServiceMaster	Dyno-Rod	Wimpy	Total
GCE No qualification obtained	20 (64.5)	17 (54.8)	24 (46.2)	61 (53.5)
Non-response	— —	2 (6.5)	2 (3.8)	4 (3.5)

TABLE 2. *Main occupations of franchisees prior to entry into franchising*

	ServiceMaster		Dyno-Rod		Wimpy		Total	
		%		%		%		%
Manual	6	19.4	3	9.7	5	9.6	14	12.3
Lower level white collar	1	3.2	1	3.2	3	5.8	5	4.4
Supervisor to middle management/semi- professional	16	51.6	13	41.9	13	25.0	42	36.8
Higher managerial/ professional	2	6.5	2	6.5	2	3.8	6	5.3
Self-employed	5	16.1	11	35.5	25	48.1	41	36.0
Other/NR	1	3.2	1	3.3	4	7.7	6	5.3
	$N=31$	100.0	$N=31$	100.0	$N=52$	100.0	$N=114$	100.0

TABLE 3. *Reasons for taking up a franchise*

	ServiceMaster		Dyno-Rod		Wimpy		Total	
		%		%		%		%
An opportunity to have own business and still be part of a national organisation	14	45.2	13	41.9	7	13.5	34	29.8
To make money/sound business venture	4	12.9	6	19.4	8	15.4	18	15.8
Less risky than starting in business on your own because of proven product/service and technical "know how" available/easy to run/ready-made market	8	25.8	8	25.8	13	25.0	29	25.4

TABLE 3. *(cont.)*

	ServiceMaster		Dyno-Rod		Wimpy		Total	
Opportunity to build a business for the future and/or family	1	3.2	—	—	1	1.9	2	1.7
Greater job satisfaction	2	6.5	1	3.2	—	—	3	2.6
Had appropriate experience or related business	2	6.5	1	3.2	4	7.7	7	6.1
Other	—	—	2	6.5	4	7.7	6	5.3
Non-response	—	—	—	—	15	28.6	15	13.2
	$N=31$	100.0	$N=31$	100.0	$N=52$	100.0	$N=114$	100.0

TABLE 4. *Would respondents be otherwise self-employed if they had not taken up franchises?*

	ServiceMaster		Dyno-Rod		Wimpy		Total	
		%		%		%		%
Yes	20	64.5	24	77.4	—	—	44	71.0
No	7	22.6	3	9.7	—	—	10	16.1
Don't Know	2	6.5	1	3.2	—	—	3	4.8
Non-response	2	6.5	3	9.7	—	—	5	8.1
	$N=31$	100.0	$N=31$	100.0	—	—	$N=62$	100.0

TABLE 5. *How franchisees first approached their franchisors about buying a franchise*

	ServiceMaster		Dyno-Rod		Wimpy		Total	
		%		%		%		%
In response to an advertisement for franchisees	15	48.4	17	54.8	8	15.4	40	35.1
Contacted the franchisor directly or via a Franchisee after using an outlet or service	4	12.9	6	19.4	29	55.8	39	34.2
Attended a franchise exhibition	—	—	1	3.2	—	—	1	0.9
Other	12	38.7	7	22.6	13	25.0	32	28.1
Non-response	—	—	—	—	2	3.9	2	1.8
	$N=31$	100.0	$N=31$	100.0	$N=52$	100.0	$N=114$	100.0

TABLE 6. *Did respondents feel they were given full financial information before signing their franchise contracts*

	ServiceMaster		Dyno-Rod		Wimpy		Total	
		%		%		%		%
Yes	23	74.2	27	87.1	41	78.9	91	79.8
No	8	25.8	3	9.7	9	17.3	20	17.5
Non-response	—	—	1	3.2	2	3.9	3	2.6
	$N=31$	100.0	$N=31$	100.0	$N=52$	100.0	$N=114$	100.0

TABLE 7. *Respondents' feelings, prior to signing a franchise contract, on the franchisors' prediction of likely profits*

Franchisor	ServiceMaster		Dyno-Rod		Wimpy		Total	
		%		%		%		%
Grossly overestimated likely profits	2	6.5	4	12.9	5	9.6	11	9.7
Overestimated likely profits	8	25.8	13	41.9	12	23.1	33	29.0
Neither overestimated nor underestimated profits	17	54.8	9	29.0	23	44.2	49	43.0
Underestimated likely profits	3	9.7	5	16.1	5	9.6	13	11.4
Grossly underestimated likely profits	—	—	—	—	2	3.9	2	1.8
Non-response	1	3.2	—	—	5	9.6	6	5.3
	$N=31$	100.0	$N=31$	100.0	$N=52$	100.0	$N=114$	100.0

TABLE 8. *Did respondents consult a solicitor or other adviser before signing their franchise contracts?*

	ServiceMaster		Dyno-Rod		Wimpy		Total	
		%		%		%		%
Solicitor:								
Yes	11	35.5	25	80.7	31	59.6	67	58.8
No	20	64.5	6	19.4	18	34.6	44	38.6
Non-response	—	—	—	—	3	5.8	3	2.6
	$N=31$	100.0	$N=31$	100.0	$N=52$	100.0	$N=114$	100.0
Other adviser								
Yes	11	35.5	17	54.8	12	23.1	40	35.1

TABLE 8. (*cont.*)

	ServiceMaster		Dyno-Rod		Wimpy		Total	
No	20	64.5	14	45.2	26	50.0	60	52.6
Non-response	—	—	—	—	14	26.9	14	12.3
	$N=31$	100.0	$N=31$	100.0	$N=52$	100.0	$N=114$	100.0

TABLE 9. *Party from whom franchisees purchased their franchises*

	ServiceMaster		Dyno-Rod		Wimpy		Total	
		%		%		%		%
Directly from the franchisor	24	77.4	23	74.2	30	57.7	77	67.5
Directly from another franchisee	7	22.6	8	25.8	20	38.5	35	30.7
Other	—	—	—	—	—	—	—	—
Non-response	—	—	—	—	2	3.9	2	1.8
	$N=31$	100.0	$N=31$	100.0	$N=52$	100.0	$N=114$	100.0

TABLE 10. *Decision on site or area location made by*

	ServiceMaster		Dyno-Rod		Wimpy		Total	
		%		%		%		%
The franchisor	7	22.6	9	29.0	19	36.5	35	30.7
The franchisee himself	22	71.0	17	54.8	25	48.1	64	56.1
Other	1	3.2	5	16.1	4	7.7	10	8.8
Non-response	1	3.2	—	—	4	7.7	5	4.4
	$N=31$	100.0	$N=31$	100.0	$N=52$	100.0	$N=114$	100.0

TABLE 11. *Owner of franchisees business premises*

	ServiceMaster		Dyno-Rod		Wimpy		Total	
		%		%		%		%
The franchisor	1	3.2	—	—	—	—	1	0.9
The franchisee	20	64.5	15	48.4	4	7.7	39	34.2
Owned by a third party	8	25.8	16	51.6	46	88.5	70	61.4
Non-response	2	6.5	—	—	2	3.9	4	3.5
	$N=31$	100.0	$N=31$	100.0	$N=52$	100.0	$N=114$	100.0

TABLE 12. *Average number of hours per week worked by franchisees*

	ServiceMaster		Dyno-Rod		Wimpy		Total	
		%		%		%		%
Less than 30 hours	—	—	1	3.2	2	3.9	3	2.6
30–40 hours	—	—	2	6.5	3	5.8	5	4.4
40–45 hours	4	12.9	—	—	4	7.7	8	7.0
45–50 hours	9	29.0	6	19.4	4	7.7	19	16.7
50–55 hours	5	16.1	7	22.6	2	3.9	14	12.3
55–60 hours	4	12.9	5	16.1	6	11.5	15	13.2
60–65 hours	6	19.4	3	9.7	8	15.4	17	14.9
65–70 hours	1	3.2	2	6.5	4	7.7	7	6.1
70–75 hours	1	3.2	3	9.7	7	13.5	11	9.7
75–80 hours	—	—	1	3.2	2	3.9	3	2.6
80–85 hours	1	3.2	1	3.2	3	5.8	5	4.4
85–90 hours	—	—	—	—	1	1.9	1	0.9
90 hours or more	—	—	—	—	2	3.9	2	1.8
Non-response	—	—	—	—	4	7.7	4	3.5
	$N=31$	100.0	$N=31$	100.0	$N=52$	100.0	$N=114$	100.0

TABLE 13. *Extent of assistance provided by wife*

	ServiceMaster		Dyno-Rod		Wimpy		Total	
		%		%		%		%
"However and whenever needed"	11	35.5	6	19.4	14	26.9	31	27.2
Less than 10 hours	1	3.2	2	6.5	2	3.9	5	4.4
10–20 hours	3	9.7	1	3.2	—	—	4	3.5
20–30 hours	4	12.9	2	6.5	3	5.8	9	7.9
30–40 hours	2	6.5	2	6.5	2	3.9	6	5.3
40–45 hours	1	3.2	—	—	3	5.8	4	3.5
45–50 hours	—	—	—	—	1	1.9	1	0.9
50 hours or more/full-time	4	12.9	2	6.5	2	3.9	8	7.0
Other	—	—	1	3.2	1	1.9	2	1.6
None	5	16.1	15	48.4	24	46.2	44	38.6
	$N=31$	100.0	$N=31$	100.0	$N=52$	100.0	$N=114$	100.0

TABLE 14. *Did franchisees think that the public with whom they have contact understand their relationship with the franchisor?*

	ServiceMaster		Dyno-Rod		Wimpy		Total	
		%		%		%		%
Yes	5	16.1	1	3.2	8	15.4	14	12.3
No	24	77.4	29	93.6	38	73.1	91	79.8
Other/don't know	—	—	1	3.2	2	3.9	3	2.6
Non-response	2	6.5	—	—	4	7.7	6	5.3
	$N=31$	100.0	$N=31$	100.0	$N=52$	100.0	$N=114$	100.0

TABLE 15. *How do the public think of franchisees?*

	ServiceMaster		Dyno-Rod		Wimpy		Total	
		%		%		%		%
As an independent operator	6	19.4	6	19.4	5	9.6	17	14.9
As someone working for a larger organisation	16	51.6	23	74.2	38	73.1	77	67.5
"Some understand, some not"	6	19.4	2	6.5	1	1.9	9	7.9
As both independent and working for larger organisation	1	3.2	—	—	3	5.8	4	3.5
Other	—	—	—	—	—	—	—	—
Non-response	2	6.5	—	—	5	9.6	7	6.1
	$N=31$	100.0	$N=31$	100.0	$N=52$	100.0	$N=114$	100.0

TABLE 16. *Quality of formal training*

	ServiceMaster		Dyno-Rod		Wimpy		Total	
		%		%		%		%
Excellent	3	9.7	2	6.5	9	17.3	14	12.3
Good	8	25.8	5	16.1	6	11.5	19	16.7
Reasonable	13	41.9	12	38.7	15	28.9	40	35.1
Not very good	4	12.9	1	3.2	3	5.8	8	7.0
Poor	3	9.7	4	12.9	2	3.9	9	7.9
Franchisor does not provide/not applicable	—	—	5	16.1	7	13.5	12	10.5
Non-response	—	—	2	6.5	10	19.2	12	10.5
	$N=31$	100.0	$N=31$	100.0	$N=52$	100.0	$N=114$	100.0

TABLE 17. *Quality of equipment supplied by franchisor*

	ServiceMaster		Dyno-Rod		Wimpy		Total	
		%		%		%		%
Excellent	10	32.3	10	32.3	14	26.9	34	29.8
Good	11	35.5	11	35.5	12	23.1	34	29.8
Reasonable	8	25.8	8	25.8	9	17.3	25	21.9
Not very good	1	3.2	—	—	1	1.9	2	1.8
Poor	1	3.2	—	—	2	3.9	3	2.6
Franchisor does not provide/not applicable	—	—	—	—	5	9.6	5	4.4
Non-response	—	—	2	6.5	9	17.3	11	9.7
	$N=31$	100.0	$N=31$	100.0	$N=52$	100.0	$N=114$	100.0

TABLE 18. *Quality of supplies sold by franchisor to franchisees*

	ServiceMaster		Dyno-Rod		Wimpy		Total	
		%		%		%		%
Excellent	11	35.5	7	22.6	14	26.9	32	28.1
Good	17	54.8	10	32.3	15	28.9	42	36.8
Reasonable	3	9.7	7	22.6	16	30.8	26	22.8
Not very good	—	—	1	3.2	1	1.9	2	1.8
Poor	—	—	—	—	—	—	—	—
Franchisor does not provide/not applicable	—	—	3	9.7	—	—	3	2.6
Non-response	—	—	3	9.7	6	11.5	9	7.9
	$N=31$	100.0	$N=31$	100.0	$N=52$	100.0	$N=114$	100.0

TABLE 19. *Quality of operating manual/s*

	ServiceMaster		Dyno-Rod		Wimpy		Total	
		%		%		%		%
Excellent	19	61.3	5	16.1	14	26.9	38	33.3
Good	8	25.8	10	32.3	13	25.0	31	27.2
Reasonable	4	12.9	8	25.8	9	17.3	21	18.4
Not very good	—	—	2	6.5	4	7.7	6	5.3
Poor	—	—	3	9.7	2	3.9	5	4.4
Franchisor does not provide/not applicable	—	—	1	3.2	5	9.6	6	5.3
Non-response	—	—	2	6.5	5	9.6	7	6.1
	$N=31$	100.0	$N=31$	100.0	$N=52$	100.0	$N=114$	100.0

TABLE 20. *Quality of national advertising*

	ServiceMaster		Dyno-Rod		Wimpy		Total	
		%		%		%		%
Excellent	3	9.7	5	16.1	8	15.4	16	14.0
Good	9	29.0	3	9.7	9	17.3	21	18.4
Reasonable	8	25.8	12	38.7	15	28.9	35	30.7
Not very good	3	9.7	4	12.9	4	7.7	11	9.7
Poor	3	9.7	5	16.1	7	13.5	15	13.2
Franchisor does not provide/not applicable	5	16.1	1	3.2	3	5.8	9	7.9
Non-response	—	—	1	3.2	6	11.5	7	6.1
	$N=31$	100.0	$N=31$	100.0	$N=52$	100.0	$N=114$	100.0

TABLE 21. *Quality of book-keeping assistance/advice*

	ServiceMaster		Dyno-Rod		Wimpy		Total	
		%		%		%		%
Excellent	2	6.5	1	3.2	2	3.9	5	4.4
Good	7	22.6	4	12.9	3	5.8	14	12.3
Reasonable	12	38.7	7	22.6	6	11.5	25	21.9
Not very good	1	3.2	1	3.2	2	3.9	4	3.5
Poor	1	3.2	6	19.4	4	7.7	11	9.7
Franchisor does not provide/not applicable	8	25.8	10	32.3	26	50.0	44	38.6
Non-response	—	—	2	6.5	9	17.3	11	9.7
	$N=31$	100.0	$N=31$	100.0	$N=52$	100.0	$N=114$	100.0

TABLE 22. *Quality of technical support*

	ServiceMaster		Dyno-Rod		Wimpy		Total	
		%		%		%		%
Excellent	4	12.9	4	12.9	—	—	8	12.9
Good	8	25.8	4	12.9	—	—	12	19.4
Reasonable	9	29.0	14	45.2	—	—	23	37.1
Not very good	3	9.7	1	3.2	—	—	4	6.5
Poor	3	9.7	7	22.6	—	—	10	16.1
Franchisor does not provide/not applicable	3	9.7	—	—	—	—	3	4.8
	1	3.2	1	3.2	—	—	2	3.2
	$N=31$	100.0	$N=31$	100.0	—	—	$N=62$	100.0

TABLE 23. *Quality of day-to-day business advice*

	ServiceMaster		Dyno-Rod		Wimpy		Total	
		%		%		%		%
Excellent	3	9.7	1	3.2	7	13.5	11	9.7
Good	7	22.6	9	29.0	7	13.5	23	20.2
Reasonable	10	32.3	8	25.8	8	15.4	26	22.8
Not very good	2	6.5	1	3.2	5	9.6	8	7.0
Poor	2	6.5	5	16.1	10	19.2	17	14.9
Franchisor does not provide/not applicable	7	22.6	5	16.1	6	11.5	18	15.8
Non-response	—	—	2	6.5	9	17.3	11	9.7
	$N=31$	100.0	$N=31$	100.0	$N=52$	100.0	$N=114$	100.0

TABLE 24. *Availability of franchisor for advice*

	ServiceMaster		Dyno-Rod		Wimpy		Total	
		%		%		%		%
Excellent	8	25.8	12	38.7	—	—	20	32.3
Good	12	38.7	8	25.8	—	—	20	32.3
Reasonable	5	16.1	3	9.7	—	—	8	12.9
Not very good	5	16.1	2	6.5	—	—	7	11.3
Poor	—	—	5	16.1	—	—	5	8.1
Franchisor does not provide/not applicable	1	3.2	—	—	—	—	1	1.6
Non-response	—	—	1	3.2	—	—	1	1.6
	$N=31$	100.0	$N=31$	100.0	—	—	$N=62$	100.0

TABLE 25. *Franchising enables you to own and develop a business more speedily than starting a business on your own account*

	ServiceMaster		Dyno-Rod		Wimpy		Total	
		%		%		%		%
Strongly agree	13	41.9	18	58.1	—	—	31	50.0
Agree	13	41.9	11	35.5	—	—	24	38.7
Neither agree nor disagree	4	12.9	1	3.2	—	—	5	8.1
Disagree	—	—	—	—	—	—	—	—
Strongly disagree	1	3.2	1	3.2	—	—	2	3.2
Non-response	—	—	—	—	—	—	—	—
	$N=31$	100.0	$N=31$	100.0	—	—	$N=62$	100.0

TABLE 26. *Franchising enables you to own and develop a business with less risk than starting a business on your own account*

	ServiceMaster		Dyno-Rod		Wimpy		Total	
		%		%	%			%
Strongly agree	8	25.8	11	35.5	—	—	19	30.7
Agree	15	48.4	10	32.3	—	—	25	40.3
Neither agree nor disagree	4	12.9	4	12.9	—	—	8	12.9
Disagree	1	3.2	1	3.2	—	—	2	3.2
Strongly disagree	3	9.7	4	12.9	—	—	7	11.3
Non-response	—	—	1	3.2	—	—	1	1.6
	$N=31$	100.0	$N=31$	100.0	—	—	$N=62$	100.0

TABLE 27. *How well known did franchisees think their franchise company's brand-name was?*

	ServiceMaster		Dyno-Rod		Wimpy		Total	
		%		%	%			%
Very well known	6	19.4	17	54.8	—	—	23	37.1
Well known	2	6.5	3	9.7	—	—	5	8.1
Fairly well known	12	38.7	4	12.9	—	—	16	25.8
Not very well known	8	25.8	2	6.5	—	—	10	16.1
Hardly known	1	3.2	—	—	—	—	1	1.6
Not known	—	—	2	6.5	—	—	2	3.2
Don't know	—	—	—	—	—	—	—	—
Non-response	2	6.5	3	9.7	—	—	5	8.1
	$N=31$	100.0	$N=31$	100.0	—	—	$N=62$	100.0

TABLE 28. *How important did franchisees feel their brand-name was to the success of their business?*

	ServiceMaster		Dyno-Rod		Wimpy		Total	
		%		%	%			%
Very important	22	71.0	28	90.3	—	—	50	80.7
Important	2	6.5	—	—	—	—	2	3.2
Fairly important	1	3.2	1	3.2	—	—	2	3.2
Makes little difference	—	—	—	—	—	—	—	—
Not very important	3	9.7	—	—	—	—	3	4.8
Not important	1	3.2	—	—	—	—	1	1.6
Don't know	—	—	—	—	—	—	—	—
Non-response	2	6.5	2	6.5	—	—	4	6.5
	$N=31$	100.0	$N=31$	100.0	—	—	$N=62$	100.0

TABLE 29. *Did franchisees believe their businesses were more successful because they were franchised?*

		ServiceMaster		Dyno-Rod	Wimpy		Total	
		%		%	%		%	
More successful	25	80.7	25	80.7	—	—	50	80.7
Less successful	2	6.5	4	12.9	—	—	6	9.7
Other/don't know	3	9.7	—	—	—	—	3	4.8
Non-response	1	3.2	2	6.5	—	—	3	4.8
	$N=31$	100.0	$N=31$	100.0	—	—	$N=62$	100.0

TABLE 30. *What did franchisees feel were the main advantages of franchising to themselves?*

	ServiceMaster		Dyno-Rod		Wimpy		Total	
	N	%	N	%	N	%	N	%
Independence/an opportunity to run own business	2	6.5	5	16.1	5	9.6	12	10.5
Benefit of a well-known protected tradename	11	35.5	17	54.8	20	38.5	48	42.1
Less capital risk	1	3.2	2	6.5	3	5.8	6	5.3
Backing of a large organisation/training, advice, etc.	20	64.5	13	41.9	21	40.4	54	47.4
National advertising	7	22.6	11	35.5	12	23.1	30	26.3
Security	—	—	1	3.2	3	5.8	4	3.5
Standard formula for presentation and quality	—	—	—	—	10	19.2	10	8.8
Other	6	19.4	1	3.2	5	9.6	12	10.5

TABLE 31. *What did franchisees feel were the main disadvantages of franchising to themselves?*

	ServiceMaster		Dyno-Rod		Wimpy		Total	
	N	%	N	%	N	%	N	%
Tight control of franchisor via the contract	5	16.1	11	35.5	16	30.8	32	28.1
Royalties	16	51.6	15	48.4	15	28.9	46	40.4
Not truly independent	5	16.1	8	25.8	3	5.8	16	14.0
Remote from franchisor	1	3.2	1	3.2	2	3.9	4	3.5

TABLE 31. (*cont.*)

	ServiceMaster		Dyno-Rod		Wimpy		Total	
	N	%	N	%	N	%	N	%
Lack of direction and leadership by franchisor	2	6.5	—	—	1	1.9	3	2.6
National tradename could be tarnished by bad franchisees	1	3.2	—	—	5	9.6	6	5.3
Other	1	3.2	2	6.5	5	9.6	8	7.0
None	5	16.1	3	9.7	9	17.3	17	14.9

TABLE 32. *How did franchisees feel about their businesses?*

	ServiceMaster		Dyno-Rod		Wimpy		Total	
		%		%		%		%
I am satisfied with my present franchise	20	64.5	21	67.7	37	71.2	78	68.4
I would prefer a franchise dealing with a different product/service	—	—	—	—	—	—	—	—
I would prefer to be a completely independent operator in a similar business to the one I have now	8	25.8	8	25.8	10	19.2	26	22.8
I would prefer to be a completely independent operator in a different business	2	6.5	1	3.2	1	1.9	4	3.5
I would prefer not to be in business for myself whether franchised or not	1	3.2	—	—	2	3.9	3	2.6
Non-response	—	—	1	3.2	2	3.9	3	2.6
	$N=31$	100.0	$N=31$	100.0	$N=52$	100.0	$N=114$	100.0

TABLE 33. *In franchisees' opinions, which of the following statements most accurately describe their contracts?*

	ServiceMaster		Dyno-Rod		Wimpy		Total	
		%		%		%		%
Weighted very much in favour of franchisor	13	41.9	11	35.5	11	21.2	35	30.7

TABLE 33. *(cont.)*

	ServiceMaster		Dyno-Rod		Wimpy		Total	
Weighted moderately in favour of franchisor	11	35.5	9	29.0	17	32.7	37	32.5
Weighted slightly in favour of franchisor	3	9.7	9	29.0	13	25.0	25	21.9
Weighted slightly in favour of franchisee	2	6.5	1	3.2	2	3.9	5	4.4
Weighted moderately in favour of franchisee	—	—	—	—	1	1.9	1	0.9
Weighted very much in favour of franchisees	1	3.2	—	—	1	1.9	2	1.8
Other	1	3.2	1	3.2	—	—	2	1.8
Non-response	—	—	—	—	7	13.5	7	6.1
	N=31	100.0	*N*=31	100.0	*N*=52	100.0	*N*=114	100.0

TABLE 34. *Understanding by franchisees of their right to sell their franchise*

	ServiceMaster		Dyno-Rod		Wimpy		Total	
		%		%		%		%
Franchisee does not have the right to sell his franchise	1	3.2	—	—	4	7.7	6	4.4
Franchisee may sell but only to his franchisor	1	3.2	3	9.7	—	—	3	3.5
Franchisee may sell to an approved person but his franchisor has the right of first refusal	4	12.9	7	22.6	4	7.7	15	13.2
Franchisee may sell to anyone who is approved by his franchisor	23	74.2	19	61.3	34	65.4	76	66.7
Franchisee may sell to anyone without his franchisor's approval	1	3.2	1	3.2	7	13.5	9	7.9
Don't know	1	3.2	—	—	—	—	1	0.8
Non-response	—	—	1	3.2	3	5.8	4	3.5
	N=31	100.0	*N*=31	100.0	*N*=52	100.0	*N*=114	100.0

TABLE 35. *Had franchisors ever expressed an interest in buying-back?*

	ServiceMaster		Dyno-Rod		Wimpy		Total	
		%		%		%		%
Yes	1	3.2	3	9.7	—	—	4	3.5
No	30	96.8	27	87.1	44	84.6	101	88.6
Non-response	—	—	1	3.2	8	15.4	9	7.9
	N=31	100.0	*N*=31	100.0	*N*=52	100.0	*N*=114	100.0

TABLE 36. *Had franchisees ever threatened to terminate franchisees' contracts?*

	ServiceMaster		Dyno-Rod		Wimpy		Total	
		%		%		%		%
Yes	3	9.7	5	16.1	2	3.9	10	8.8
No	27	87.1	25	80.7	46	88.5	98	86.0
Non-response	1	3.2	1	3.2	4	7.7	6	5.3
	N=31	100.0	*N*=31	100.0	*N*=52	100.0	*N*=114	100.0

TABLE 37. *Provided the franchisor is willing, do franchisees plan to renew their contracts when they expire?*

	ServiceMaster		Dyno-Rod		Wimpy		Total	
		%		%		%		%
Yes	24	77.4	22	71.0	32	61.5	78	68.4
No	1	3.2	4	12.9	5	9.6	10	8.8
Don't know	3	9.7	2	6.5	3	5.8	8	7.0
Non-response	3	9.7	3	9.7	12	23.1	18	15.8
	N=31	100.0	*N*=31	100.0	*N*=52	100.0	*N*=114	100.0

TABLE 38. *Franchisee's income in last paid employment before taking current franchise*

	ServiceMaster		Dyno-Rod		Wimpy		Total	
		%		%		%		%
Under £1,500 p.a.	3	9.7	2	6.5	4	7.7	9	7.9
£1,500–£2,000	10	32.3	4	12.9	6	11.5	20	17.5
£2,000–£2,500	9	29.0	4	12.9	7	13.4	20	17.5
£2,500–£3,000	2	6.5	3	9.7	1	19.2	15	13.2
£3,000–£4,000	1	3.2	8	25.8	4	7.7	13	11.4
£4,000–£5,000	3	9.7	4	12.9	2	3.9	9	7.9

TABLE 38. (*cont.*)

	ServiceMaster		Dyno-Rod		Wimpy		Total	
£5,000–£7,000	2	6.5	2	6.5	1	1.9	5	4.4
£7,000–£10,000	1	3.2	—	—	1	1.9	2	1.8
£10,000–£15,000	—	—	—	—	2	3.9	2	1.8
£15,000 and over	—	—	2	6.5	—	—	2	1.8
Non-response	—	—	2	6.5	15	28.8	17	14.9
	$N=31$	100.0	$N=31$	100.0	$N=52$	100.0	$N=114$	100.0

TABLE 39. *Approximate level of gross sales for 1975*

	ServiceMaster		Dyno-Rod		Wimpy		Total	
		%		%		%		%
Less than £10,000 p.a.	10	33.0	1	3.2	—	—	11	9.7
£10,000–£20,000	4	12.9	1	3.2	1	1.9	6	5.3
£20,000–£30,000	4	12.9	7	22.6	5	9.6	16	14.0
£30,000–£40,000	—	—	4	12.9	3	5.8	7	6.1
£40,000–£50,000	1	3.2	1	3.2	3	5.8	5	4.4
£50,000–£70,000	—	—	4	12.9	3	5.8	7	6.1
£70,000–£100,000	—	—	4	12.9	1	1.9	5	4.4
£100,000–£150,000	—	—	2	6.5	2	3.9	4	3.5
£150,000 or over	—	—	1	3.2	—	—	1	0.9
Non-response	12	38.7	6	19.4	34	65.4	52	45.6
	$N=31$	100.0	$N=31$	100.0	$N=52$	100.0	$N=114$	100.0

TABLE 40. *Approximate level of gross profits for 1975*

	ServiceMaster		Dyno-Rod		Wimpy		Total	
		%		%		%		%
Less than £5,000 p.a.	4	12.9	1	3.2	—	—	5	4.4
£5,000–£10,000	2	6.5	2	6.5	2	3.9	6	5.3
£10,000–£15,000	1	3.2	1	3.2	—	—	2	1.8
£15,000–£20,000	1	3.2	4	12.9	3	5.8	8	7.0
£20,000–£30,000	1	3.2	2	6.5	3	5.8	6	5.3
£30,000–£50,000	—	—	3	9.7	3	5.8	6	5.3
£50,000–£70,000	—	—	—	—	—	—	—	—
£70,000–£100,000	—	—	—	—	1	1.9	1	0.9
£100,000 or over	—	—	—	—	—	—	—	—
Non-response	22	71.0	18	58.1	40	76.9	80	70.2
	$N=31$	100.0	$N=31$	100.0	$N=52$	100.0	$N=114$	100.0

TABLE 41 *Approximate level of net profits for 1975*

	ServiceMaster		Dyno-Rod		Wimpy		Total	
		%		%		%		%
Less than £5,000 p.a.	11	35.5	6	19.4	7	13.5	24	21.1
£5,000–£10,000	3	9.7	4	12.9	6	11.5	13	11.4
£10,000–£15,000	1	3.2	4	12.9	3	5.8	8	7.0
£15,000–£20,000	—	—	2	6.5	—	—	2	1.8
£20,000–£30,000	—	—	1	3.2	—	—	1	0.9
£30,000–£50,000	—	—	—	—	—	—	—	—
£50,000–£70,000	—	—	—	—	—	—	—	—
£70,000–£100,000	—	—	—	—	—	—	—	—
£100,000 or over	—	—	—	—	—	—	—	—
Non-response	16	51.6	14	45.2	36	69.2	66	57.9
	$N=31$	100.0	$N=31$	100.0	$N=52$	100.0	$N=114$	100.0

TABLE 42. *Amount that franchisees took out of their business in 1975*

	ServiceMaster		Dyno-Rod		Wimpy		Total	
		%		%		%		%
Less than £1,500 p.a.	3	9.7	2	6.5	6	11.5	11	9.7
£1,500–£2,000	1	3.2	3	9.7	3	5.8	7	6.1
£2,000–£2,500	9	29.0	4	12.9	9	17.3	22	19.3
£2,500–£3,000	4	12.9	2	6.5	3	5.8	9	7.9
£3,000–£4,000	6	19.4	5	16.1	5	9.6	16	14.0
£4,000–£5,000	2	6.5	6	19.4	4	7.7	12	10.5
£5,000–£7,000	2	6.5	1	3.2	4	7.7	7	6.1
£7,000–£10,000	1	3.2	3	9.7	—	—	4	3.5
£10,000–£15,000	—	—	1	3.2	—	—	1	0.9
£15,000 or more	—	—	—	—	1	1.9	1	0.9
Other	—	—	—	—	1	1.9	1	0.9
Non-response	3	9.7	4	12.9	16	30.8	23	20.2
	$N=31$	100.0	$N=31$	100.0	$N=52$	100.0	$N=114$	100.0

TABLE 43. *Level of satisfaction of franchisees with the profitability of their businesses*

	ServiceMaster		Dyno-Rod		Wimpy		Total	
		%		%		%		%
Very satisfied	3	9.7	5	16.1	4	7.7	12	10.5
Satisfied	15	48.4	12	38.7	15	28.9	42	36.8
Neither satisfied nor dissatisfied	4	12.9	10	32.3	16	30.8	30	26.3

TABLE 43. (cont.)

	ServiceMaster		Dyno-Rod		Wimpy		Total	
Dissatisfied	5	16.1	1	3.2	12	23.1	18	15.8
Very dissatisfied	2	6.5	3	9.7	3	5.8	8	7.0
Non-response	2	6.5	—	—	2	3.9	4	3.5
	$N=31$	100.0	$N=31$	100.0	$N=52$	100.0	$N=114$	100.0

TABLE 44. *For anyone who is willing to work hard in Britain it is possible to create a successful and profitable business*

	ServiceMaster		Dyno-Rod		Wimpy		Total	
		%		%		%		%
Strongly agree	14	45.2	19	61.3	16	30.8	49	43.0
Agree	11	35.5	8	25.8	18	34.6	37	32.5
Neither agree nor disagree	3	9.7	2	6.5	2	3.9	7	6.1
Disagree	—	—	—	—	3	5.8	3	2.6
Strongly disagree	2	6.5	2	6.5	10	19.2	14	12.3
Non-response	1	3.2	—	—	3	5.8	4	3.5
	$N=31$	100.0	$N=31$	100.0	$N=52$	100.0	$N=114$	100.0

Part Two
Responses of Franchisees Participating in the Depth-Interview Programme

Section One: *The Decision to Become Self-employed*

1. *Did Franchisees really understand what franchising involved when they first contacted ServiceMaster/Dyno-Rod/Wimpy?*

	ServiceMaster		Dyno-Rod		Wimpy		Total	
		%		%		%		%
Yes	8	53.3	11	68.8	9	45.0	28	54.9
No	7	46.7	5	31.3	11	55.0	23	45.1
	$N=15$	100.0	$N=16$	100.0	$N=20$	100.0	$N=51$	100.0

2. *Did the availability of capital influence franchisees' decision to take a franchise rather than set up a totally independent business?*

	ServiceMaster		Dyno-Rod		Wimpy		Total	
		%		%		%		%
Yes	10	66.7	6	37.5	4	20.0	20	39.2
No	5	33.3	10	62.5	16	80.0	31	60.8
	N=15	100.0	*N*=16	100.0	*N*=20	100.0	*N*=51	100.0

3. *What was the approximate time gap between decision to become self-employed and taking up a franchise?*

	ServiceMaster		Dyno-Rod		Wimpy		Total	
		%		%		%		%
Up to 1 year	13	86.7	12	75.0	16	80.0	41	80.4
1–2 years	1	6.7	1	6.3	2	10.0	4	7.8
More than 2 years	—	—	2	12.5	1	5.0	3	5.9
Other	1	6.7	1	6.3	1	5.0	3	5.9
	N=15	100.0	*N*=16	100.0	*N*=20	100.0	*N*=51	100.0

4. *Was their present franchise the only one that franchisees considered?*

	ServiceMaster		Dyno-Rod		Wimpy		Total	
		%		%		%		%
Yes	13	86.7	11	68.8	17	85.0	41	80.4
No	2	13.3	5	51.3	3	15.0	10	19.6
	N=15	100.0	*N*=16	100.0	*N*=20	100.0	*N*=51	100.0

5. *Did franchisees consider any alternative forms of self-employment?*

	ServiceMaster		Dyno-Rod		Wimpy		Total	
		%		%		%		%
Yes	7	46.7	6	37.5	6	30.0	19	37.3
No	8	53.3	9	56.3	12	60.0	29	56.9
Other (already self-employed)	—	—	1	6.3	2	10.0	3	5.9
	N=15	100.0	*N*=16	100.0	*N*=20	100.0	*N*=51	100.0

6. *If they had not gone into franchising did Franchisees feel they would still be working for themselves?*

	ServiceMaster		Dyno-Rod		Wimpy		Total	
		%		%		%		%
Yes	9	60.0	9	56.3	16	80.0	34	66.7
No	6	40.0	7	43.8	4	20.0	17	33.3
	$N=15$	100.0	$N=16$	100.0	$N=20$	100.0	$N=51$	100.0

7. *Have their businesses fulfilled their original ambitions?*

	ServiceMaster		Dyno-Rod		Wimpy		Total	
		%		%		%		%
Yes	*12	80.0	13	81.3	13	65.0	38	74.5
No	3	20.0	3	18.8	7	35.0	13	25.5
	$N=15$	100.0	$N=16$	100.0	$N=20$	100.0	$N=51$	100.0

* Includes: "partly" and "commencing to".

8. *Would they advise anyone else to do what they have done?*

	ServiceMaster		Dyno-Rod		Wimpy		Total	
		%		%		%		%
Yes	11	73.3	15	93.8	19	95.0	45	89.2
No	2	13.3	1	6.3	1	5.0	4	7.8
Other	2	13.3	—	—	—	—	2	3.9
	$N=15$	100.0	$N=16$	100.0	$N=20$	100.0	$N=51$	100.0

9. *Did franchisees feel, taking into account both the benefits and difficulties associated with being their own boss, that self-employment was worthwhile?*

	ServiceMaster		Dyno-Rod		Wimpy		Total	
		%		%		%		%
Yes	*14	93.3	15	93.8	18	90.0	47	92.2
No	1	6.7	**1	6.3	1	5.0	3	5.9
Other	—	—	—	—	1	5.0	1	2.0
	$N=15$	100.0	$N=16$	100.0	$N=20$	100.0	$N=51$	100.0

*Includes 2 personally "yes", financially "no".
** Same "no" as question 11.

10. *Did franchisees experience sufficient freedom within terms of their franchise agreement to really feel they were working for themselves?*

	ServiceMaster		Dyno-Rod		Wimpy		Total	
		%		%		%		%
Yes	11	73.3	13	81.3	15	75.0	39	76.5
No	4	26.7	3	19.8	5	25.0	12	23.5
	$N=15$	100.0	$N=16$	100.0	$N=20$	100.0	$N=51$	100.0

11. *Did franchisees still feel their original decision to go into franchising was the right one?*

	ServiceMaster		Dyno-Rod		Wimpy		Total	
		%		%		%		%
Yes	15	100.0	16	100.0	19	95.0	50	98.0
No	—	—	—	—	1	5.0	1	2.0
	$N=15$	100.0	$N=16$	100.0	$N=20$	100.0	$N=51$	100.0

12. *If franchisees were starting in business again today would they still go into franchising?*

	ServiceMaster		Dyno-Rod		Wimpy		Total	
		%		%		%		%
Yes	10	66.7	13	81.3	14	70.0	37	72.5
No	5	33.3	3	18.8	6	30.0	14	27.5
	$N=15$	100.0	$N=16$	100.0	$N=20$	100.0	$N=51$	100.0

13. *How long did franchisees think they would continue in their present businesses?*

	ServiceMaster		Dyno-Rod		Wimpy		Total	
		%		%		%		%
Indefinitely	8	53.3	14	87.5	12	60.0	34	66.7
Other	7	46.7	2	12.5	8	40.0	17	33.3
	$N=15$	100.0	$N=16$	100.0	$N=20$	100.0	$N=51$	100.0

Section Two: Relationships with Others

14. *Did franchisees encounter any problems in their relationships with their franchisors?*

	ServiceMaster		Dyno-Rod		Wimpy		Total	
		%		%		%		%
Yes	9	60.0	4	25.0	9	45.0	22	43.1
No	6	40.0	12	75.0	11	55.0	29	56.9
	$N=15$	100.0	$N=16$	100.0	$N=20$	100.0	$N=51$	100.0

15. *Did franchisees feel that their franchisor gave a fair service for the return he got from them?*

	ServiceMaster		Dyno-Rod		Wimpy		Total	
		%		%		%		%
Yes	9	60.0	11	68.8	13	65.0	33	64.7
No	6	40.0	5	31.3	7	35.0	18	35.3
	$N=15$	100.0	$N=16$	100.0	$N=20$	100.0	$N=51$	100.0

16. *Did franchisees think the public was generally aware that ServiceMaster/Dyno-Rod/Wimpy was franchised?*

	ServiceMaster		Dyno-Rod		Wimpy		Total	
		%		%		%		%
Yes	—	—	2	12.5	3	15.0	5	9.8
No	15	100.0	14	87.5	17	85.0	45	90.2
	$N=15$	100.0	$N=16$	100.0	$N=20$	100.0	$N=51$	100.0

If "yes" did they think it affected their attitude towards franchisees' businesses?

Yes	—	1	1	2
No	—	—	—	—

17. *Did franchisees think their franchisors made any attempt to inform the public that ServiceMaster/Dyno-Rod/Wimpy was franchised?*

	ServiceMaster		Dyno-Rod		Wimpy		Total	
		%		%		%		%
Yes	4	26.7	2	56.3	1	5.0	7	13.7

TABLE 17. (cont.)

	ServiceMaster		Dyno-Rod		Wimpy		Total	
No	11	73.3	14	87.5	19	95.0	44	86.3
	N = 15	100.0	N = 16	100.0	N = 20	100.0	N = 51	100.0

18. *Did franchisees' customers generally realise that they worked for themselves?*

	ServiceMaster		Dyno-Rod		Wimpy		Total	
		%		%		%		%
Yes	*6	40.0	*3	18.8	8	40.0	17	33.3
No	8	53.3	13	81.3	11	55.0	32	62.7
Other	1	6.7	—	—	1	5.0	2	3.9
	N = 15	100.0	N = 16	100.0	N = 20	100.0	N = 51	100.0

* Regular customers, i.e. large companies, generally realised they worked for themselves or were told.

If "no" did they tell them?

Yes	3	—	1	4
No	4	13	10	27
	7	13	11	31

19. *How well did franchisees think their brand name was known to:*
    (a) *The general public:*

	ServiceMaster		Dyno-Rod		Wimpy		Total	
		%		%		%		%
Well known	2	13.3	15	93.8	20	100.0	37	72.5
Not well known	13	86.7	1	6.3	—	—	14	27.5
	N = 15	100.0	N = 16	100.0	N = 20	100.0	N = 51	100.0

    (b) *Their potential customers:*

	ServiceMaster		Dyno-Rod		Wimpy		Total	
		%		%		%		%
Well known	4	26.7	13	81.3	20	100.0	37	72.5
Not well known	11	73.3	3	18.8	—	—	14	27.5
	N = 15	100.0	N = 16	100.0	N = 20	100.0	N = 51	100.0

20. *Was the brand name ServiceMaster/Dyno-Rod/Wimpy important to franchisees' businesses?*

	ServiceMaster		Dyno-Rod		Wimpy		Total	
		%		%		%		%
Yes	10	66.7	15	93.8	17	85.0	42	82.4
No	4	26.7	1	6.3	2	10.0	7	13.7
Other/DK	1	6.7	—	—	1	5.0	2	3.9
	$N=15$	100.0	$N=16$	100.0	$N=20$	100.0	$N=51$	100.0

21. *In franchisees' opinions, were their businesses more successful as a result of being franchised than they would otherwise have been?*

	ServiceMaster		Dyno-Rod		Wimpy		Total	
		%		%		%		%
Yes	12	80.0	14	87.5	14	70.0	40	78.4
No	3	20.0	1	6.3	4	20.0	8	15.7
Other/DK	—	—	1	6.3	2	10.0	3	5.9
	$N=15$	100.0	$N=16$	100.0	$N=20$	100.0	$N=51$	100.0

22. *Did franchisees feel that there was less risk in running a franchised business than in running a totally independent business?*

	ServiceMaster		Dyno-Rod		Wimpy		Total	
		%		%		%		%
Yes	10	66.7	15	93.8	13	65.0	38	74.5
No	5	33.3	1	6.3	6	30.0	12	23.5
Other/DK	—	—	—	—	1	5.0	1	2.0
	$N=15$	100.0	$N=16$	100.0	$N=20$	100.0	$N=51$	100.0

23. *Did franchisees have employees working for them?*

	ServiceMaster		Dyno-Rod		Wimpy		Total	
		%		%		%		%
Yes	10	66.7	16	100.0	20	100.0	46	90.2
No	5	33.3	—	—	—	—	5	9.8
	$N=15$	100.0	$N=16$	100.0	$N=20$	100.0	$N=51$	100.0

24. *Did franchisees find the task of organising other people satisfying?*

	ServiceMaster		Dyno-Rod		Wimpy		Total	
		%		%		%		%
Yes	6	40.0	14	87.5	14	70.0	34	66.7
No	2	13.3	2	12.5	5	20.0	9	17.6
Other	—	—	—	—	1	5.0	1	2.0
Non-response/ Not applicable	7	46.7	—	—	—	—	7	13.7
	$N=15$	100.0	$N=16$	100.0	$N=20$	100.0	$N=51$	100.0

25. *Did franchisees have problems obtaining staff?*

	ServiceMaster		Dyno-Rod		Wimpy		Total	
		%		%		%		%
Yes	5	33.3	3	18.8	5	25.0	13	25.5
No	3	20.0	13	81.3	15	75.0	31	60.8
Non-response/ Not applicable	7	46.7	—	—	—	—	7	13.7
	$N=15$	100.0	$N=16$	100.0	$N=20$	100.0	$N=51$	100.0

26. *Did their employees know they were franchisees?*

	ServiceMaster		Dyno-Rod		Wimpy		Total	
		%		%		%		%
Yes	8	53.3	16	100.0	20	100.0	44	86.3
No	—	—	—	—	—	—	—	—
Non-response/ Not applicable	7	46.7	—	—	—	—	7	13.7
	$N=15$	100.0	$N=16$	100.0	$N=20$	100.0	$N=51$	100.0

If "yes" did this affect their attribute to working for them?

		%		%		%		%
Yes	—	—	3	18.8	1	5.0	4	9.1
No	8	100.0	11	68.8	19	95.0	38	86.4
Other	—	—	2	12.5	—	—	2	4.5
	$N=8$	100.0	$N=16$	100.0	$N=20$	100.0	$N=44$	100.0

27. *Did franchisees experience any problems in their relationship with customers?*

	ServiceMaster		Dyno-Rod		Wimpy		Total	
		%		%		%		%
Yes	1	6.7	4	25.0	—	—	5	9.8
No	14	93.3	12	75.0	*20	100.0	46	90.2
	$N=15$	100.0	$N=16$	100.0	$N=20$	100.0	$N=51$	100.0

* Occasionally.

Section Three: Advantages and Disadvantages of Franchising

28. *Were there any aspects of franchising that franchisees did not like?*

	ServiceMaster		Dyno-Rod		Wimpy		Total	
		%		%		%		%
Yes	12	80.0	15	93.8	16	80.0	43	84.3
No	3	20.0	1	6.3	4	20.0	8	15.7
	$N=15$	100.0	$N=16$	100.0	$N=20$	100.0	$N=51$	100.0

29. *Were there any benefits franchisees' customers got from them as a franchise that they would not have got from an ordinary managed branch of a large company?*

	ServiceMaster		Dyno-Rod		Wimpy		Total	
		%		%		%		%
Yes	14	93.3	16	100.0	15	75.0	45	88.2
No	1	6.7	—	—	5	25.0	6	11.8
	$N=15$	100.0	$N=16$	100.0	$N=20$	100.0	$N=51$	100.0

30. *Were there any ways in which franchisees could perhaps have given their customers an even better service but could not because of restrictions in their agreements with their franchiser?*

	ServiceMaster		Dyno-Rod		Wimpy		Total	
		%		%		%		%
Yes	5	33.3	*1	6.3	10	50.0	16	31.4
No	10	66.7	15	93.8	10	50.0	35	68.6
	$N=15$	100.0	$N=16$	100.0	$N=20$	100.0	$N=51$	100.0

* Reduce cost.

Conclusion

Though this research was only essentially an exploratory study into franchising in Britain, it does indicate that when a franchise system is based upon a good and market-tested product or service, the franchisee can achieve his goal of self-employment more rapidly and with less risk than would be the case if he staged his entry into self-employment by more conventional means.

On the other hand, viewing the situation from the viewpoint of the franchisor, franchising offers the prospect of rapid growth with limited capital. In addition, any company attempting to cope with geographically dispersed markets with all the communications, motivational, and labour problems frequently involved may find that franchising has much to offer.

Whilst the difficulties facing the small business continue to receive wide publicity, there appears to be no decline in the number of people wishing to be self-employed. Besides the tax advantages associated with self-employment, other rewards of a non-economic nature, e.g. independence, autonomy, and self-expression, often rate highly with the self-employed. The above research indicated that a good franchise can satisfy most of these desires.

Index